# FRIDAY NIGHT LIGHTS

*Untold Stories from*

*Behind the Lights*

## Dr. Nathanial Hearne

TOUCH
PUBLISHING

Cover photo and author photos by Dorothy Sammons Photography

ISBN: 978-0-9911511-0-3 [softcover print]
ISBN: 978-0-9911511-1-0 [hardcover print]
ISBN: 978-0-9911511-3-4 [eBook]
ISBN: 978-0-9911511-2-7 [study guide]
ISBN: 978-0-9911511-4-1 [DVD]

Published by Touch Publishing
Requests should be directed to:
P.O. Box 180303
Arlington, Texas 76096
www.TouchPublishingServices.com

Library of Congress Control Number: 2014934083

Printed in the United States of America on acid-free paper

# Dedication

This book could not have been written apart from the love, support, strength, and wisdom of my wife, Callie; my parents, Olean and Rayfield Hearne; and my brothers and sisters, Evelyn, Rayfield Jr., Mittie, Gloria, Jackie, Kenneth, and Debbie.

They have all given me the strength and encouragement to confront, articulate, and embrace my past experiences, and compile those experiences into this book. I also want to thank my children, stepchildren, grandchildren, and my many nieces and nephews for the inspiration they gave me to write this book. I love you all!

# Acknowledgements

*Friday Night Lights: Untold Stories from Behind the Lights* is the result of the wisdom and generosity of many people: Among them my parents, siblings, children, relatives, and a number of friends.

Over the past 40 years, I have had the good fortune to coach, teach, preach, mentor, and serve as an administrator at a number of public schools and religious institutions across the state of Texas. I would like to thank the athletes, students, parents, and educators I encountered along the way. You were a major influence and encouragement in my decision to write this book.

My editors / publishers, David and Kim Soesbee, did an impressive job of bringing together the fragmented pieces of a manuscript into clear ideas that were central to helping shape this book. A great debt of gratitude goes to Callie, my precious wife. She encouraged me to write this book, repeatedly discussed with me ideas to incorporate, and helped shape and re-shape it.

Dr. Gene and Lois Nini, thank you for your friendship and love through the years.

Finally, I am grateful to God. He gave me life; He gave me a dream; and He brought me into my purpose. He trained me up, for each of you. And for that, I am deeply indebted!

# Table of Contents

*Coach Hearne was a teacher, coach, &
administrator at Permian High School
in Odessa, Texas for 10 years.*

# Introduction

I have been connected with the Church and public schools in the state of Texas for more than three decades. In those thirty-plus years, there is a tragedy I've seen happen over and over again. Students fail to reach their maximum potential and do not grow up to become responsible contributing members of our society.

I have watched and listened as, one by one, students paraded through my office with stories of defeat, rejection, and outright abandonment—stories of how they were cast aside by their parents, ignored by their peers, and rejected by the Church, their schools, and society as a whole.

Though the students were of different ethnicities and their situations not always the same, they had two things that linked them together: troubled relationships in the home, and a lack of knowledge of Jesus the Christ.

Through much assessment of the experiences I've had, and analysis of the types of repeating problems I've seen through the years, I've come to believe that if those in leadership will change the standards by which they measure success, there will be a profoundly positive impact on the development of our country's children.

Being a former athlete and participating in organized sports on the high school and college level, both as a coach and a player, I've seen success measured in a variety of ways. Many sports teams, especially those with winning traditions, have rules, guidelines, or beliefs they have woven into the very fabric of their organization from top to bottom. These rules are often placed in a team handbook that is presented to the players and referred to by the coaching staff as the "bible" for that particular team.

Players are then coached to believe in this Team Bible philosophy. They are taught to encourage their teammates to believe in and have faith in the system; practice hard and everyone will experience miraculous success. The trophy or championship rides on whether or not the Team Bible is followed.

During my years of involvement with organized sports teams, including football, basketball, track, and baseball, I've had the pleasure of participating both as a player and a coach on a number of championship teams that used this philosophy. I call this philosophy *secular success*. Secular success is determined and measured by natural, human standards. There are objective guidelines that players follow that are spelled out clearly. Adherence to the Team Bible and this measure of secular success can, indeed, help win championships. But rarely do the goals measured by secular success address the long-term, inner character development of the athlete. The goals are focused on the immediacy of the competition season.

Lasting success is only possible when we submit ourselves to God's Word and become followers of Jesus Christ in word and in deed. When a leader includes God's principles within his or her action plans, there will not only be secular success, but *biblical success* as well. It is through achieving personal biblical success that one can effectively lead and guide others, best preparing them for success in life.

I've tried to live my life against the standards God has placed before me. I believe that, with Jesus the Christ who strengthens me, nothing is impossible to achieve. When you connect those kinds of beliefs with hard work, it will always produce positive results. These are the beliefs I have attempted to instill in the many students I've encountered as a teacher, an administrator, and as a pastor, and to the athletes I've coached.

I've spent the better part of twenty years coaching a nexus of different athletic teams. One opportunity God blessed me with was coaching football at Permian High School in Odessa, Texas.

During my time as an assistant coach in the football program at Permian, I was fortunate to have been part of the State Championship team that was also named National Champions in 1989, and the State Championship team in 1991. Both of these teams had perfect seasons, which, at that time, was an accomplishment made by only one other team in the history of Texas high school football on the Class 5A level—The 1985 Houston Yates team.

Permian had a tremendous reputation for winning football championships (1965, 1972, 1980, 1984, 1989, and 1991). In those days, they were the epitome of high school football success. They were so well-known, that in 1988 an author came to Odessa to follow us through our football season that year with the intent of writing a book about us. That book, *Friday Night Lights*, made the New York Times Top Ten Bestseller List.

In December 2004, a major motion picture based on the book was released. According to an article in *Sports Illustrated* magazine, the *Friday Night Lights* movie was ranked as one of the top ten best sports movies ever made.[1] Public opinion of the movie, according to national reviews, was so favorable that two years later a television show was created and it became an Emmy Award-winning series.

From my experiences in coaching, the accolades bestowed upon those young men during that time and the championship teams they played on, came as a direct result of their belief in the philosophy of secular success. Since 1965, the rallying cry for

Permian has been "MOJO." For a Permian Panther, MOJO encapsulates everything strong and successful about Permian. Adherence to the MOJO tradition and success go hand-in-hand.

Now, I'm not advocating that having a secular success goal is all bad. As a coach, I am fully aware of the importance and crucial value of a solid game plan. What I am saying is this: Over the years, many of the students and players—of all ethnicities—I've had the opportunity to work with in classrooms and sporting arenas all across the state of Texas, have told me later how valuable those beliefs I taught them regarding biblical success have been in their lives.

I've been given many opportunities to build biblical success into those around me. I've served as a teacher, coach, and administrator at Permian High School and in a number of schools across the state. For fifteen years, I served as pastor of several different Methodist churches. In this book I share with you many of those stories. I also chronicle my personal struggles as a child growing up in a segregated society  There is much to learn from my self-awareness of how others treated me, and how I responded. I grew up in poverty, and those experiences gave me first-hand knowledge of what it's like to live in at-risk conditions—not knowing where the next meal was coming from, heading off to school each day with patches on my clothes and holes in my shoes, and not knowing from month to month if my family would be evicted from our home. Being in those situations taught me the importance of recognizing the advantages of disadvantage and the disadvantage of advantages that living for Jesus will bring. You will see how I later then taught advantages of faith in Christ Jesus to the students I encountered to help them achieve eternal success.

Ultimately, this book is about training our children in the core values that make up their character and helping them to think differently when faced with perceived disadvantages in life. No matter who they are: at-risk kids, honor students, students with special needs, dropouts, athletes, or general population students, they must be taught to believe that there is no mountain too high to climb and no valley too deep to emerge from. I really do believe that in the United States of America, no child should be left behind.

If you are someone who is serious about improving our American society, if you are serious about doing your part to educate our children so they are properly prepared as this nation's next generation, then begin here with me by making a serious commitment to training yourself in the knowledge of biblical success. You will then be equipped to go into your circle of influence in the home, in the classroom, or on the field, and build a legacy of character into our youth that will last a lifetime.

# PART 1:
# My MOJO Stories

*Coach Hearne speaks to the University
of Indiana Hoosiers football team.*

# Chapter 1
# Behind the Lights

*"Only Nate Hearne had a different perspective on it all. His struggle to keep Boobie on the team when he had tried to walk out the door during halftime against the Rebels wasn't some act. He understood the psychological pain Boobie was going through, how unimaginably hard it was to sit there and watch someone else perform with brilliance a role that had once been his."*

*- Friday Night Lights* by H.G. Bissinger[1]

In the description of his best-selling book *How Children Succeed: Grit, Curiosity, and the Hidden Power of Character*, author Paul Tough asks the question, "Why do some children succeed while others fail?" He recognizes: "The story we usually tell about childhood success is the one about intelligence: success comes to those who score highest on tests, from preschool admissions to SATs." Tough contends that the qualities which matter most in the development, and ultimately the success of our nation's youth, have more to do with character: skills like perseverance, curiosity, conscientiousness, optimism, and self-control.[2]

Society as a whole tends to look at character as something innate and unchanging; a core set of attributes that define one's essence. But in *Character, Strengths and Virtues*, a handbook of human strengths and virtues by Martin Seligman and Christopher Peterson, character is defined in a similar way as Tough described. These two professors of positive psychology agree that character involves a set of abilities or strengths that are very much changeable—entirely malleable skills that can be learned, practiced, and taught.[3]

This is a concept that I wholeheartedly agree with. I agree with it because I've experienced it with my students and athletes. Young people often have a strong influence or situation from their past that threatens to destroy their present and future. I have found that character can be developed when a leader intentionally shows them they don't have to be shaped by past hurts or by the culture around them. As leaders, we must show young people that they can be shaped by the vision of who they want to become. Here are a couple of situations where I had to put this concept into practice.

## Halftime with Boobie

The prologue of Friday Night Lights by H.G. "Buzz" Bissinger opens with Permian High School's football team playing against Midland Lee in a district championship game. James Miles, a senior running back who everyone knew simply as "Boobie," is on the sidelines because of a knee injury that required surgery. He was injured in a scrimmage game at Jones Stadium in Lubbock, Texas early in that school year.

Chris Comer, Boobie's replacement, had turned out to be a pleasant surprise that season. During the district game, he scored on a 77-yard touchdown run. Boobie was watching all of this from the sideline—a position he was not familiar with up until that year. And he did not like it. That whole football season had been rough for Boobie, and he was still rehabbing his knee. During his playing career, Boobie had always been in the limelight. He never had to stand on the sidelines in any sport.

As I watched Boobie throughout the first half of the game, I could tell by his body language that watching the game was becoming increasingly painful for him emotionally. Boobie had experienced a very difficult childhood. His mother abandoned him. His father started seeing another woman and it was reported that she abused him. Boobie was removed from the home and placed initially in foster care, and then later placed in the custody of his uncle, L.V. Miles, who lived in Odessa, Texas.

The pain Boobie experienced while in the foster care system left him with deep emotional wounds. There weren't many adults he trusted.

When halftime of the Midland Lee game came, I watched Boobie exit the field with his head down and shoulders slumped, walking dejectedly to the dressing room. Before this season, this behavior would have been strange to anyone who knew him. Boobie was always high-energy during the games because he was the star. Boobie was an exceptional all-around athlete. I knew this because as a sophomore, he played basketball for me on the junior varsity team. You could say he was a smaller version of the NBA's LeBron James, before there was a LeBron James. He was 6'1", weighed 195 pounds, and was very muscular. He could handle a basketball with either hand while running at full speed. He was quick, agile, and a leaper. He averaged twenty points a game his sophomore year. He had no fear in his heart, and was very confident in his abilities. I loved coaching him and watching him play the game.

However, that day in the locker room, Boobie ripped his gear off and starting throwing it around the showers. The heartache and broken spirit he felt had reached a climax. I knew that was going to be it for him. I also knew none of the other coaches would try to stop him or try to calm him down. They had witnessed this behavior before, and they knew he wouldn't respond positively to them. His reaction to them was very different from how he reacted to me. Whereas Boobie never showed me any disrespect, sometimes he would become aggressive with them—almost to the point of a physical confrontation. If I was around, I would always step in between Boobie and the other coach, and I would look Boobie in the eyes. In his tight, piercing gaze, I knew in those moments Boobie didn't recognize his coaches as advocates. Instead, he saw them as adults—foster parents who hurt him—and he didn't trust them. He was trying to protect himself from the pain.

His blowup at halftime was an extension of his great pain. And I knew I needed to be the one to stop him. I had watched him during the first half, and I knew he couldn't continue to hide the embarrassment and anguish swelling inside of him. It certainly didn't help that the coaching staff was raving about Comer. Boobie couldn't hold it any longer. All this rage inside of him had to be released.

I went to him and looked straight into his eyes. I said, "Boobie, you don't want to do this. You have too much to lose if you continue to act like this. You can get through this."

I could tell he didn't want to relax. He didn't want to concede to his perceived failure.

To get Boobie to put his uniform back on, walk back out of the locker room, and stand on the sideline again, when his world was crumbling around him, was a major accomplishment. But, he did it out of respect and loyalty to me. I had spent a lot of time building a relationship with Boobie. I knew he was operating at a huge disadvantage, but I was hoping we could turn that disadvantage into an advantage for him. Boobie knew I wasn't going to harm him in any way. He trusted me.

My goal was to get Boobie to see he still had a future. He needed to be patient, control his temper, and hang in there. I hoped to get him to see his value to the team so that when we made it to the playoffs, it would all be worth the wait.

If Comer continued gaining the yards he was averaging, and we could supplement them with Boobie's ability to block and carry the ball, not a single team in the playoffs would want to face Chris Comer and Boobie Miles in the same backfield. In my opinion, having him healthy for the playoffs would be a major plus for us.

It was painful for me to watch him. I was willing to work with him in any capacity. I had been through three knee surgeries of my own. I knew what it would take for him to rehab that knee.

*My success with Boobie came because he knew that I loved and cared for him as a person, not just as a football player. I reminded him of his future, helping him to see beyond what was going on in the moment.*

To this day, Boobie calls me. If he didn't view me as an advocate, as someone who loved him unconditionally, he would never do that.

When I spent time with Boobie, I always attempted to accomplish two things—first, I wanted to affirm him for who he was as a person. Second, I wanted him to know that the love I had in my heart for him outweighed any negative behavior he exhibited. There would be consequences, but it would never stop me from loving him unconditionally. Boobie knew that.

**A Promise to L.V.**

When Boobie came up from junior high to Permian as a sophomore football player, L.V. Miles called and asked if I would keep an eye on his nephew. He knew how fragile Boobie was, and that he needed someone to be an advocate for him. He needed someone he could trust during difficult times. I made L.V. a promise that I would take care of Boobie.

In *Friday Night Lights*, Bissinger wrote that in reply to the question, "What would Boobie be without football?" One of the coaches reportedly responded, "A big ol' dumb nigger."

The day the book was released, L.V. called me and asked if I had read the book. I hadn't yet. He said, "You're the hero, you need to read it." Then he asked if I would find out which coach called Boobie a "dumb nigger."

"L.V., if a coach on the staff said that, they're not going to come right out and tell me they said it," I told him.

"I understand," he said dejectedly.

"But I promise you, I'll ask," I told him.

He responded, "That's all I want."

Shortly after my conversation with L.V., we had a staff meeting. With all the coaches present, I asked who referred to Boobie as a "dumb nigger." As I expected, no one confessed. The following Monday morning, as I was preparing for my biology class, a teacher walked into my classroom and asked if I had a minute.

"I heard you were looking for the coach who called Boobie the dumb nigger," she said.

I told her, yes, that I had inquired about it.

She said, with smug sarcasm, "It's your running buddy, your workout buddy! Mike Belew said it."

I thanked the teacher, and she turned and walked out.

What I had just heard caught me by surprise. Not so much for who had allegedly made the comment, but that the teacher even knew I had asked about it. I had only asked the question in the one meeting with the coaching staff. I had not mentioned anything to anyone else.

A lot of different scenarios began to formulate in my mind. In my handling of this delicate situation, I learned some important principles for dealing with a potentially explosive dilemma.

First, I assessed what I knew to be true about Mike's character. I had spent a lot of time with Mike over the years. The teacher was right. We were workout partners. For several years, we either ran or lifted weights together every day during the season. The time I spent with Mike had given me more than ample opportunity to gain insight into his character.

I knew Mike's character to be that of a good man with a good heart. He wasn't mean-spirited. He had a deep compassion and empathy for others. I had never doubted that assessment of him. I had witnessed him going the extra mile for several black players on the team on numerous occasions, for things which had nothing to do with winning football games.

Second, Mike was an excellent coach, but I knew he struggled with how to communicate effectively with Boobie. I surmised that if Mike had spoken those words to Buzz, they were said out of frustration. As I mentioned, the strongholds in Boobie's life made him difficult to coach. Boobie didn't trust most adults. He had come from an environment where either he was abused or abandoned by many central adult figures in his life.

Once, during a playoff game, Boobie had taped three rally towels to the belt on his uniform. Boobie thought this made him look cool. Mike thought it to be a bad idea because the defense could use the towels to pull him down. It would put Boobie at a disadvantage.

Boobie was going through pre-game warm-ups and Mike came to me and said, "Coach, I have a problem. Look at Boobie. He's got all those rally towels taped to his belt. That's not good."

Instantly, I knew what Mike wanted.

I got a pair of scissors from the trainer. Then, I called Boobie to me and said, "Boobie we need you to rush for 200 yards today, and you can't do it with all these towels taped to your uniform. The defense will use these towels to drag you down."

I cut the towels off and he ran back out to his warm-up position without a word of protest. With Mike, more than likely, it would have been a different story. Coaching Boobie was much different from any other running back Mike had ever coached.

Third, I took into account where Mike had come from. Mike had been raised in West Texas, where the "N" word was used as commonly as shaking salt on a steak. Mike's perception of the things Buzz would encounter spending a year in Odessa with the team was much different from my perception. When I was interviewed by Buzz, I knew he was an intelligent man and a gifted writer. Many of the questions he asked, I perceived as being already tainted with the overt racial overtones he had experienced during his time in the city.

Growing up in a racially intense environment all my life made me keenly aware of those things. I knew, without question, that Buzz would be given a full-frontal view of these racial tensions as he conducted his research for the book. When I answered his questions, I wanted to be truthful and speak my heart. However, I was careful not to say things out of anger or frustration that I would later regret.

Now, to be clear, Mike has never told me he said it. My belief is that if he did, Mike made a mistake. He was not aware Buzz had picked up on those racially insensitive things from the community that would become the focal point of his book. Mike spoke out of this unawareness.

Mike retired after a long, productive coaching and teaching career. We have been friends for over twenty-five years. I've both stayed at his house and had dinner with his family on several occasions. Likewise, he has stayed in my home. As you can tell, I know him well. Because I am an ordained minister, I even had the honor of performing his wedding vows. By the way, Mike's wife is black.

As happens to all of us from time to time, Mike likely spoke out of careless frustration. Was it my place to condemn him? In Luke 6:37-38, Jesus said, *"Do not judge, and you will not be judged. Do not condemn and you will not be condemned. Forgive and you will be forgiven." (NIV)*

I've made many mistakes in my life, as have we all. God and those who love me have forgiven me a multitude of errors. I never had any condemnation for Mike, and no desire to sit in judgment of his life.

After considering all of these points, I knew that I was not going to pass that information on to L.V., because nothing good could come of it. Boobie and L.V. had already suffered enough. My presenting that information to them would only add salt to a gaping wound. They both needed time to heal.

## The Word I Don't Like

After the teacher left my room that day, there was another pressing matter I knew I would have to address. It would cause conscious restraints in how I dealt with the "dumb nigger" issue. It was the painful, but factual, dynamic of the black athletes on the team calling each other the "N" word. The black athletes frequently used the word in casual conversation with each other and with white athletes on the team. The coaches on the staff, the white players, and the Hispanic players on the team all heard the black players use the "N" word in conversations on numerous occasions. The "N" word was the big white elephant in the room.

And now, the fact that it had been written in a book and whites were using it as well, made it potentially catastrophic to our team dynamics.

How was I to deal with this conundrum? I was the only black coach on staff and I knew the black players used it in their conversations. Before any of this happened, I had already been approached by whites who asked: "If they're using it, what makes it so offensive when we use it?"

Throughout my coaching career the "N" word has been a painful subject for me. It was frustrating and humiliating to hear black players using that word in the company of their peers, no matter what their peers' skin color. It is a word that has no place in our common language. I tried to address this issue with the black athletes at Permian long before *Friday Night Lights* was ever released. Every black player on the football team knew how I felt about them using the "N" word. Whether in the locker room, the classroom, the hallways, on the practice field, or during games, I did not permit it.

Every year, at the beginning of the football season, the head junior varsity coach held a meeting with all the sophomore football players. This meeting was equivalent to an orientation in Permian football etiquette. After my first attendance at one of these meetings, I knew I needed to have a separate orientation with the black athletes. The things the black players really needed to hear were not addressed by the white coaches. I took the initiative to tell them what they needed to know. This may be the reason Buzz, the coaches, teachers, and community viewed me as the "handler of the blacks" on the team.

The first, and most important issue I addressed was the use of the "N" word. I forbade it at any time during their career as players or students at Permian High School. I threatened them with severe consequences if I heard it.

When I walked into the locker room, I would overhear them say to one another, "Here comes Coach Hearne. You better watch your mouth!" Sometimes, they would see me coming and playfully say, "Coach Hearne," then they would point at a teammate and say, "He's using that word you don't like."

But they all knew it was serious business with me.

During the mid-1980s, the use of the "N" word by the rap culture had risen to new heights. Recording artists were using the word like wildcatters drilling for oil in West Texas during the Boom. The more holes they punched in the ground, the richer they became. The more profusely and profoundly rappers incorporated the "N" word into their music, the quicker they skyrocketed to fame and fortune. Using the "N" word had become profitable business.

Growing up in the '50s and '60s, my experience with the "N" word was so much different than it was for the young black athletes I was coaching. I knew it would be a challenge to get them to see how degrading it was to use that word, when this new explosion of rap artists grew bigger and louder each day. They were dancing to it and playing it in their cars. They were hearing and seeing it in rap videos on television. No doubt they wondered how it was a bad thing.

It was a challenge! But they respected me enough not to use it in my presence. The message I wanted to get across to them was to take pride in who they were and how they conducted themselves as black athletes on the team. I wanted them to see what a golden opportunity it was to be a player on this team. Permian had a deep, rich history, and a strong winning tradition. Their program was known not only statewide, but nationally. I wanted them to realize that excelling in the program would open doors that could lead to a bright future.

I challenged them to be the very best they could be. I wanted them to give full effort every day in the classroom, on the practice field, and during the games. No whining, no complaining. If they did everything the teachers and coaches asked of them, they would have a better chance to make it in a world filled with racial tension, personal struggles, and pain.

I had no doubt they could do it. They were bright and gifted young men. But I had to keep the vision in front of them every day. I couldn't let up. I was not going to joke with them about using that word. It was that important to me. If I didn't assume that responsibility, no one else would. If I didn't try to help them understand, I was doing a disservice to them, their parents, the community, and all the future players coming into the program.

My motivation, and the message I wanted so desperately to convey, was that they had an opportunity to become men of character. I wanted them to know if they used the "N" word in the presence of their white teammates, they were disrespecting and diminishing themselves as men. I told them in that initial sophomore meeting, and as often as needed afterward, that if they wanted to be respected later in life by their peers, they had to start by conducting themselves as men of character, both on the field and in the classroom.

I reminded them that they wouldn't be football players forever—that one day they would grow up to be men, husbands, fathers, and leaders. And when they encountered their former white teammates with their wives and children, men who would likely also be doctors, businessman, lawyers, or dentists, they would want to be respected and remembered not because they could run fast or catch a football, but for how they carried and conducted themselves off the field—as men of character.

# Chapter 2
# A Welcome Surprise

Joshua 1:8 is one of three places in the Bible where the Hebrew word *taskil* (taś·kîl), translated to "success" or "successful" is used:

*"Keep this book of the Law always on your lips; meditate on it day and night, so that you may be careful to do everything written in it. Then you will be prosperous and **successful**."*
*(NIV - emphasis mine)*

It doesn't take a rocket scientist to see that this is a clear-cut formula for anyone who wants to succeed in life. Staying connected to what God's way of doing things and receiving God's blessings go hand-in-hand. In fact, that combination is the only formula that's guaranteed to work. Anything else is a gamble, and chances are anyone who tries to succeed any other way (in other words, apart from God's guidance) is likely to fail.

When you look at it that way, it's not hard to put your finger on the principles connected with success. The concepts are not as complex as one might think. The issue, though, is with actually living out those concepts.

That's where we, as parents, educators, and mentors, come

in. We are responsible to train up our children while they are young. It is our duty to recognize what's on the inside—the gifts, talents, skills and abilities they possess—and draw them out.

The Bible is filled with stories of individuals who started out as ordinary, unassuming people, but turned out to be outstanding heroes. They used their gifts from God to make a huge difference in many ways—displaying astounding abilities, courage, character, and wisdom—without any previous evidence that they were capable of performing such feats. I recall such a young man who I coached in football while at Permian.

If you've read *Friday Night Lights* or saw the movie, you may remember Chris Comer as one of the players highlighted in the story.

My wife, Callie, worked at Permian as a counselor during the same time I was there and at the time the events chronicled in the book and movie took place. We often talk about how Chris' character was portrayed in the movie.

It's no secret that Hollywood tends to take liberties and puts its own spin on things when writing movie scripts. After all, the more dramatic and entertaining the movie is, the more tickets they sell. And in the case of the *Friday Night Lights* movie, it was no different.

In no way am I criticizing or belittling the movie, or diminishing anything that was portrayed, but I would not be honest if I said the movie was an exact representation of what took place regarding the players on the football team, because it was not.

For example, Boobie, who I talked about in the previous chapter, was not hurt playing in a game as was implied in the movie. He was hurt during a scrimmage game at Jones Stadium in Lubbock, Texas. The way Chris Comer was portrayed in the movie was also very different from reality.

The first time I met Chris, it was quite uneventful. Coach Gary Gaines, who was the head football coach at Permian at the time, approached me one day and asked if I knew Chris Comer. The name did not ring a bell with me. He said a coach at one of the junior high schools that fed students into Permian had told him that Chris was probably someone we might want to take a look at.

He asked if I would find Chris and see if he was interested in being part of our team. As I stepped outside the field house, Ivory Christian, our All-State middle linebacker, was standing just outside the door. I asked him if he knew Chris Comer.

"Yes sir, coach, I know him," Ivory answered.

"If you see him, tell him I'm looking for him."

As I turned to walk off, the last bell rang, signaling the end of the school day. Ivory called to me, pointed to a boy exiting the school building and said, "Coach Hearne, there he is."

I waded through the mass of students and called out to Chris. I extended my hand, and said, "Hi Chris, I'm Coach Hearne." I then asked if he was planning to try out for the football team.

"Yes, sir," he answered.

It was that simple and that ordinary. That was the first time I had ever spoken to or laid eyes on Christ Comer. School had started, and he already was a student at Permian.

I make this statement because the following year, after Chris became the top back in the state, an anonymous letter was sent to 5A coaches, athletic directors, and superintendents in Midland, Abilene, and San Angelo detailing alleged recruiting violations and questionable practices that were supposedly "common knowledge in the black community." The letter specifically named me as the person doing the recruiting, and Chris Comer as one of the athletes I was supposed to have recruited. Members in the black community provided the information of my alleged recruiting activity. Although there was no truth to these allegations, this anonymous letter would ignite an investigation into Permian's off-season coaching practices that would eventually lead to me being labeled a cheater, and placed on probation by the University Interscholastic League for one year.

The movie portrayal of Chris Comer was a 180-degree difference from what the Chris Comer I coached was like. For example, Chris was not the "jitterbug-type" running back that he was shown to be on-screen. He ran north and south, and when he hit the hole, with the power and speed he possessed, he was hard to stop. His personality was not jittery either. Quite the opposite; he was so introverted that it was hard to put a read on what his true capabilities were on the football field. During the whole time I coached him, I'm sure Chris never said more than fifty words to me. And the majority of the time, those words were either "Yes sir" or "No sir."

Chris was quiet and never did things to draw attention to himself. At 5' 9" and 195 pounds, he had all the attributes that made for a good football player. But before we saw him play, I didn't know what he was capable of doing on the field.

That question was quickly put to rest when we put Chris in a game. In his first season of play as varsity running back, he rushed for nearly 800 yards in five games. Amazing!

One day a gentleman asked me about Chris.

"Comer doing pretty good?" he asked.

"Yes, he has almost 800 yards in five games," I answered.

We exchanged a little small talk, and then he asked, "Do you know who his family is?"

Odessa didn't have a large percentage of blacks. It was small enough that most everybody knew everybody. So, it wasn't surprising that he would ask such a question. But it dawned on me,

I knew very little about Chris or his family. At the time it didn't matter to me. "I think he was raised by his grandmother," I said.

"So, you don't know much about his background?" he asked.

I didn't. *Why is he asking me this?* I wondered.

In retrospect, maybe his questions were all a part of the set up for the letter.

Chris was in the spotlight, and was turning into an exceptional player. Everyone in the state had their eyes on him now. I didn't need to know anything about Chris' background. From my evaluation of him, as a coach it was obvious to me that Chris needed to be affirmed and nurtured.

Chris played "2 Technique" (Permian's terminology for a defensive tackle) on defense and was a running back on offense. To some this would seem odd, but not if you coached at Permian. We didn't depend a lot on size at the defensive tackle position. It was more about reading the stance of the offensive tackle, speed, and quickness.

To this day I believe Chris was a better defensive tackle than he was a running back. The reason I say this is because I never witnessed anyone blocking him as a 2 Technique. He was extremely quick off the ball, and many times he would be in the backfield before the quarterback could hand the ball off.

Chris was a gifted athlete, but he didn't have a very good work ethic as a sophomore player, when I started coaching him. He would show flashes of his exceptional abilities, and then he would just fade out. He wasn't in shape. He'd tire quickly because he wouldn't push himself. He didn't know how. But that was my job.

One day we were conditioning at the end of practice, and Chris was coming in last every time. He was dogging it. I knew he could do better and I decided this was the day. I wanted to know if he had heart, or if he was a quitter.

I sent the other players to the locker room and kept him behind. I ran him until he could just barely pick up his feet. He would almost stumble across the finish line and I would make him run again. When he reached the point where it looked like he was going to pass out from physical exhaustion, I stopped and told him to pick up his helmet and head to the locker room. It took him a while before he could even gather up enough energy to reach down to get his helmet. I patiently watched him labor through this process.

As he slowly, painstakingly made his way to the field house, I passed him and went on ahead to the coaches' office. As I sat in the office talking, another assistant coach came in very agitated. He said he had Comer outside waiting for me. He said he overheard Chris tell another player that he was going to get a shotgun and blow my head off.

I calmly stood and walked outside. Chris was standing there, holding his helmet in his hands with his head down. I said, "Chris, get your head up and look at me." He did.

Then I said, "Chris, I understand how you're feeling right now. I know at this very moment you feel like taking a shotgun and blowing my head off. But you need to know this:

*The reason I pushed you today, and the reason I'm going to continue to push you when I see you dogging it like that in practice, is because of the love I have in my heart for you. You have a very special gift.*

"You have a combination of size, speed, and quickness that is rare. God has truly blessed you. What I want to do is see you use that gift to its fullest potential. I don't want to see you waste it and one day regret it.

"I'm going to continue to push you until you become the best Chris Comer that God has created you to be. So, Chris, go get a shotgun, come on back and blow my head off. But, remember this," I paused and looked in his eyes, "I love you and I want nothing but the best for you. Son, I won't stop until I get it."

After that encounter, I never had a problem with Chris accepting my expectations of his abilities. He gave a full effort during practice. He was a maniac in the weight room. When he returned his junior year, during two-a-day practices I pushed him even harder. He understood, accepted, and responded. I never heard him complain again.

When we lost Boobie to injury during the scrimmage game the summer between Chris' sophomore and junior years, Chris was moved up to varsity and went on to rush for 2,000 plus yards, setting or breaking school records as we marched through the season.

In his senior year, Chris injured his knee during the fourth or fifth game of the season. I was on the sideline, watching our offense preparing to run a play and hadn't noticed that Chris got hurt. We were inside our opponent's red zone and I noticed Chris wasn't in the game. I looked around for him, thinking the head coach had, for some reason, pulled him out of the game. He wasn't standing beside the head coach. When I looked behind me, Chris was sitting on the trainer's table with his helmet off—a double "no-no" in my book.

I went over to the trainer's table and yelled at him to put his helmet back on and get back out there! He said, "Yes sir," put his helmet on, and ran back onto the field. The head trainer came up and tapped me on the shoulder.

"Coach," he said, "Chris' knee is tore up. He's torn his ACL."

"He never said a word to me about his knee," I told the trainer.

"He's not going to say anything to you about it."

That incident spoke volumes to me about Chris' personal growth. He had matured from being that sophomore who wanted to quit after every play when he grew tired, to being a senior who had the mental toughness to play with a torn ACL. (He came out of the game after the next play was run.) I know that probably sounds bad, but that's football. Chris hadn't been trained to play checkers. He was going to need that kind of character and toughness later to make it through the storms of life. In the end, Chris worked hard at his rehab, came back and rushed for 1,600 yards after only missing three games. We rode his back to a perfect 16-0 season and the school's fifth State Championship.

It's human nature when we choose someone, for whatever reason, that our assumptions of what we think that person is like always play a major role in our judgment. That's just the way we are.

Frequently, people are judged or chosen based on assumptions. If I had looked at Chris' quiet, unassuming, introverted nature and judged him based on that, I would have never discovered the God-given abilities that would make him one of the best running backs in the state. When we judge too quickly, we miss the opportunity to recognize and possibly promote some of the most gifted and talented people this world has ever seen.

It's clear from Chris' story that God doesn't make choices based on appearance. He knows that looks can be deceiving. Instead, God looks at the heart of a person. He looks inside to examine what a person is made of—their character, personality, and nature—and He judges based on what He sees there.

I have always coached players from the inside out. I've always wanted to know what's on the inside. How will they respond under pressure? What do they do when pushed to the limit? My desire in coaching athletes in this manner has nothing to do with winning games, but everything to do with producing people of character.

It is clear that God is in the business of choosing, equipping, and using people whose hearts are established in Him. Chris' heart was good. He wanted to be the best. He just didn't know how to go about making that happen. He really didn't know the sacrifices it took to be the best. That's why it's so important to nurture and affirm our children when given the opportunity. You never know what's inside the heart. It makes them better prepared to meet the challenges of this world.

Chris was a quiet, unassuming, introverted kid living in at-risk circumstances. Yet, God placed in him the natural abilities to excel on the gridiron—to do things that would astonish people.

In Proverbs 22:6, King David wrote the formula for raising our children and guiding them to successful lives. He said, *"Train up a child in the way he should go; even when he is old he will not depart from it." (ESV)*

# Chapter 3
# Handling the Black Athletes

"There was an element of Bissinger's book that shocked me and bothered me, greatly ... When I read the line about Nate Hearne, as the assistant coach 'whose primary responsibility was to handle the black players.' Really? In 1988 black players needed to be 'handled'?"

-The New York Times College Sports Blog
by Rachael Larimore[1]

Character is derived from example. I believe it is impossible to establish positive character traits without first having someone or something set as a model.

We find the evidence of this in John 15:15-16, where Jesus said to His disciples:

*"I no longer call you servants, because a servant does not know his master's business. Instead, I have called you friends, for everything I have learned from my Father I have made known to you. You did not choose me, but I chose you and appointed you so that you might go and bear fruit— fruit that will last." (NIV)*

Jesus not only was the example for His followers, but He says He learned His teachings from His Father. The fruit is the legacy left behind.

Webster defines *legacy* as "material possession or wealth left over to someone by will or bequest." Every day we contribute brushstrokes to the picture we are painting that is our legacy—who we are and how we want to be remembered. I'm of the opinion that part of our legacy is formed in the things we do when we don't think anyone is watching. Our Father sees those things, and can allow lasting fruit to come from them.

We put our legacy on display when we're given a task to complete and the person assigning the task says, "It doesn't matter how you do it, just do it."

Those who want to build a strong, healthy legacy understand the same thing I've discovered: It _always_ matters how you do it.

In others words, legacies are about our character—those skills and traits like integrity, honesty, grit, and self-discipline. Our legacy, in my opinion, has nothing to do with material possessions or wealth.

When Jesus said, "I appoint you to go out and bear fruit," He was talking about our character. When He said, "I appoint you to go out and bear fruit that will last," He was speaking of our legacy.

At the end of my first year as a junior high school coach and teacher in 1981, Mr. Joe Rutledge, who was vice principal at the school where I worked, called me to his office. He explained to me that the Ector County Independent School District (ECISD) would be making a move to desegregate their schools. He said that I might be moved to a junior high school on the north side, and I would become an assistant to one of the white coaches.

I asked him why I had to be an assistant to one of the white coaches when I was quite capable of coaching my own team. I had more than proven my abilities by beating those north-side schools in football (with only thirteen players on my team) _and_ dominating them with my basketball team.

He answered by saying, "That's just part of what we have to go through sometimes in order to get where we really want to be."

To that, I responded: "Mr. Rutledge, I've been waiting too long to coach on the high school level as it is. I have a chance to move up to Ector High at the beginning of the school year."

I continued, "Mr. Rutledge, I will not be moved over to a north side school and become a water boy when I've proven that I can coach as well as they can. I'll resign before I do that!"

Mr. Rutledge warned me to temper my spirit and just hang in there. He said, nothing had been confirmed yet. But at the same time, he was skeptical and warned against me hanging my hopes on the move to Ector High. He didn't think it would ever happen. It turns out, he was absolutely right! I was not moved up to the high school the next year. Instead, the head coach hired a white coach fresh out of college, and never even mentioned my name. I learned this news over the summer.

My older brother was a supervisor for Chevron Oil Company at the time. It was rare in those days for a black man to be in a supervisory position for a major oil company. He was intelligent, hard working, and disciplined. My brother worked his way from the bottom as a roustabout, fighting through all the racial barriers, and made it to supervisor in a relatively short period of time. It was a major accomplishment. I talked with him and he told me he could get a position for me working in the oil field, making three times the money I was making in the public schools.

When I heard that I had been passed over for the job at Ector, and after hearing all the desegregation rumors flying around the community, I decided to take my brother up on his offer. Before the summer was over, I had gone to work for Chevron Oil. And my brother was right—I was making three times the money I had made working as a teacher and coach.

But I soon discovered that was the biggest mistake I had ever made.

You see, my gifting was teaching and coaching. It was my passion. It's what came naturally to me. I'd even say coaching was in my blood. I loved working with the students and watching them mature and develop into successful, productive young men and women. It was doubly encouraging when I would later encounter those I had taught and coached and hear them say how much they had learned from me. When they thank me for being there for them during the difficult times, it is sweet for my soul.

———— 66 ————————————————

*When I was coaching or teaching, I was affirmed in how I was created. God will give us great affirmation when we do that which He created us to do. And we should be that affirming voice when we see character and strength in others.* 99 ——

It wasn't long before I wanted out of the oil field and back to coaching, but unfortunately, there were no coaching opportunities. The Boom was on and jobs were hard to find in West Texas.

One weekend, I was watching the state championship football game on television. It so happened it was between Permian and Houston Yates. I had coached several of the players on the Permian team when they were in junior high school. They were making big time contributions; three were named first team All-State at their position at the end of the season. Yates beat them soundly that day, but I was still very proud of them. They had played in back-to-back state championship games.

As I sat in my living room watching the game, I thought how awesome it would have been to coach them at Permian High School.

At the end of that season, John Wilkins resigned as head

coach and became the athletic director. Gary Gaines was named as the new Permian head football coach. I read these events in the newspaper, but I was not remotely aware my life would soon become connected to the Permian story.

## God's Mysterious Ways

God, however, knew the plans He had for me. One Saturday morning, the phone rang at my home. The person on the other end identified himself as Gary Gaines, the new head football coach at Permian High School. He stated he had a vacancy for an assistant football coach at the school and wanted to know if I would be interested in interviewing for the position.

I thought I was dreaming! I told him I would be very interested in interviewing for the position, and he asked if I would have some time that morning to talk with him.

Thirty minutes later, I was sitting in his office.

It was the first time I had ever been inside the head football coach's office at Permian. I had coached, taught in the school system, and lived in Odessa for thirty years. I never thought it would happen.

Coach Gaines impressed me as a man of character—soft-spoken—with no visible rough edges. He was a man of vision. It was often voiced in the black community that Permian would never hire a black coach. But Coach Gaines had called me. I guess "never" is a word we should be careful about using.

During the desegregation move that Mr. Rutledge had said was coming, two black coaches had been assigned to Permian. From what I understood, one coach left because he grew tired of dealing with the racial tension at the school, and the other was released because he didn't pass the state teacher's exam. In my interview, Coach Gaines said he was looking for a coach to be a role model for the black athletes at Permian. He said he had made numerous calls to people in the black community and every time he asked if they knew of someone, my name was mentioned. Coach Gaines said our meeting wasn't really much of an interview because the job was mine, if I wanted it.

When I accepted the position, I became the first black officially hired to coach football at Permian High School.

As we concluded the interview, I told Coach Gaines I was truly honored and overwhelmed by this opportunity, and that I would be more than a role model for just the black athletes. In retrospect, when I look back over my career at Permian, it's my belief I met and exceeded those self-imposed expectations.

In a blog post on *The New York Times College Sports Blog*, Brian Sweany wrote that Coach Gaines had vehemently denied he had hired me as coach primarily to "handle" the black players.[2]

Coach Gaines never once said my sole purpose in being on staff was to "handle" the black players. If I was seen in that light by anyone, it was a perception that might have been encouraged by my actions. I truly wanted them to make it and become all they were created to be.

I didn't have negative feelings toward being labeled as role model for the black athletes, and I gladly have accepted that moniker for those who have seen me in that light. But it wasn't at all how I perceived myself, or how I carried out my responsibilities.

My teaching and coaching motif was to inspire every student I encountered to greatness. To help them be more than they'd ever imagined they could be. There was no doubt in my mind that I was a good coach. Of that I was confident. It may have appeared to a casual observer that I concentrated the majority of my efforts on the black players, but that would have been a pseudo-impression. I viewed myself as a science teacher and assistant football coach at Permian who simply sought to build character and live out a legacy in all the students placed before me. It is my continuation of the legacy my seventh-grade science teacher, Mr. Clyde Haak, and my seventh-grade football coach, Coach Mark Wallace, had left for me. I'll share more about them in a later chapter.

**The Backlash**

After I resigned from my job with Chevron Oil and accepted the position as science teacher/assistant football coach at Permian, there was an uproar from the coaches at the junior high schools that fed into Permian. Some of them were pushing to get me fired before I ever had an opportunity to coach at the school. I didn't know any of them and they didn't know me—their actions were based on blind envy and jealousy.

At the time, this was one of the top coaching positions in the state. I later learned that over eighty coaches from all across Texas and outside the state had applied for the position.

One day, after being on staff for a couple of weeks, Coach Gaines called me to his office and said the Human Resource Director, Moe Madison, was there to talk to me. We met in the weight room, and he told me there were some coaches at the junior high schools who were upset that I was hired. He said they were complaining that it was unfair because I hadn't taken and passed the newly-implemented Texas Teacher Certification examination and that there were qualified coaches at the junior high schools who were more deserving of the position.

Mr. Madison said there was a possibility that I might not be able to keep the job at Permian because I hadn't taken the test. As I stood there listening to him, I could see all the social dynamics I had experienced living in a segregated society being played out in my mind. I thought to myself, *Will it ever stop?*

At that point, I said to Mr. Madison: "I've resigned from my job at Chevron and Coach Gaines said this position was mine if I wanted it. Mr. Madison, if someone is going to be without a job, it won't be me," and I walked out of the weight room.

I didn't hear anything else about it, because they had to give me the opportunity to take the state exam. If I had failed the test, I'm sure the ones who were spearheading this protest would become much more vicious with their attacks. But, they had to wait a few weeks to see what the results would be.

A couple of weeks later, I took the state exam.

During the early years, state facilitators would allow four hours to complete the test. Because the test was so easy, and I finished in one hour, I was concerned that I had done something wrong. I sat in the testing area double and triple-checking my answers for another forty-five minutes, just to make sure I was comfortable with what I turned in.

This entire episode was absolutely brainless to me. I had been out of coaching for five years working for Chevron. I didn't apply for the job, and would not have even known about the position had Coach Gaines not called me. If he had wanted any of those coaches from the junior high schools, he would have called them rather than me.

I've always wondered why any of those people never just asked Coach Gaines outright for the reason he chose to hire me instead of them.

In the Texas football coaching fraternity, you have to do your due diligence at the junior high school level before moving up to the high school ranks. I understood this, and had served at both an elementary and a junior high school for years. A few years earlier, when I was passed over for the job at Ector High School for someone who had no experience, it never occurred to me to get upset with the coach who was hired. Neither did it register to get upset with the head coaches who did the hiring. I have always operated under the belief that if they didn't want to hire me, it was their loss. I have always been confident in my abilities to find a job, because I always trusted God. I knew that as long as I worked hard and prepared myself, God would provide. And He did!

During our conversation, Moe Madison mentioned that there was a black coach at one of the feeder schools who was qualified for the job at Permian.

*If he was qualified, and working for the district, why didn't Coach Gaines hire him instead of me?* I wondered.

It was a childish attempt by others to feed the envy they felt because someone else had gotten something that they thought they deserved. Acting on envious feelings can be dangerous business.

*Those who spent copious amounts of energy trying to discredit me and get me fired, weren't really setting themselves in any better position for success. They were wasting time that could have been spent on things that were uplifting and character-building for the kids they coached.*

Instead, those kids may have been witness to a poor example of how someone should act when he doesn't get his way.

Anyone who has a desire to coach eventually wants to be a head coach. I was no different than thousands of coaches pursuing that dream. One of my biggest coaching dreams was to be a head coach and win a state championship. I had the experience to do this in both football and basketball, and I coached both of these sports at Permian.

At the end of my third year at Permian, I received a phone call during the summer from a friend, informing me of an opening for a head basketball coach position in Big Springs, a small community fifty miles east of Odessa. I applied for the position. I was called for an interview with the athletic director, who was also the head football coach at the school. The interview went well and they called me back for a second interview.

During the second interview, he said he thought I definitely had the experience to coach the team. He and the others felt I would be good for the students, the school, and the community. He said he would call me the following week to let me know his decision.

When I left his office, I had an overwhelming feeling that I was going to get the job. A couple of days later, I ran into a gentleman who worked in the athletic supply business and while in Big Springs actually had a conversation with the head coach at the school there.

"Your name came up during the visit," he told me. "They like you. You're going to get that job."

The coach in Big Springs had given me a specific date and time he would call and inform me of his choice for the position. But he didn't call that day. I was really disappointed and had a bad feeling about it. But that night I kept hoping. When he called the next day, I could tell immediately by his voice that something was wrong.

"Coach, this is probably the worst mistake I will ever make in my life, but we've decided to go with another person for the job," he said. "I'm really, really sorry about this, Coach. Good luck in the future."

I'll never forget those words. They stunned me.

God has a way of shining light on every dark situation. An outside source came to me a couple of weeks later and said, "I know the guy they hired for the position in Big Springs. He was brought in at the last minute to keep you from leaving Permian."

This was difficult news to accept, and even harder to believe. I thought, *Why would anyone keep me from improving myself, and why would anyone want to keep me at Permian?*

Coaching at Permian was one of the premier jobs in the state. That was proven by the list of candidates who applied for the position I was hired for. It was the reason those junior high coaches were so upset when I was hired. I thought my presence on the staff was not one of importance, and figured they could find a replacement for me in a heartbeat. God believed otherwise.

I've always found that in any adverse situation, setback, or disappointment in my life God had a lesson for me to learn. My job was to find the positives that He wanted me to discern in this situation. What I heard from God was to be patient and wait, because there was still important work He needed me to do at Permian.

# Chapter 4
# The UIL Ruling

---

*"Minutes earlier, after the penalties against the Permian program were announced, Hearne had lashed out at the process and its end result. But now he could only bow his head, clasp his hands and reflect on a decision that stunned most everyone involved."*

-*Odessa American,* September 21, 1990
by Garry Leavell[1]

---

James 1:2-4 reads: *"Consider it pure joy, my brothers and sisters, whenever you face trials of many kinds, because you know that the testing of your faith produces perseverence. Let perseverence finish its work so that you may be mature and complete, not lacking anything." (NIV)*

During my coaching and teaching career, I have always tried to convey that life is made up of a series of storms. The storms of life are inevitable, just like sin is inevitable. We have all sinned and fallen short, and none of us will evade the storms of life.

Throughout our lives, we will frequently find ourselves in one of three places: Getting ready to enter a storm; in the middle of a storm; or coming out of a storm. We may be tempted to let the storms of life erode our faith, but this would be a mistake. The important thing to realize is that, while you may not be able to evade a storm, it is nothing more than a test and a lesson waiting to be learned. And through that test of your faith, God wants to make you stronger. I'm well aware of the importance of viewing the storms of life with joy.

In December of 1989, we won the State Championship in football. Later that year, we were named National Champions by both the Associated Press and ESPN. When it comes to high school football, you can't get any higher than that. We were at the apex in the high school football world. But as high as we had risen, everything came tumbling down in only a matter of months.

It's a funny thing how it takes years of hard work, preparation, and commitment to rise to the top, but in just a few months' time everything can crash hard to rock bottom. At Permian, things started unraveling a little piece at a time, but then they turned into one big avalanche.

Buzz Bissinger approached the school district in 1988 about writing a book of the storied Permian High School football tradition. He was granted permission, and for the next year, he spent much time with us, gathering information for the book.

As a result of the success of his finished product, *Friday Night Lights*, Bissinger was invited to return to Odessa for a book signing. Unfortunately for him, while the book had achieved enormous success in the industry and across the nation, it was not received very well by people in some parts of the community in Odessa. It was reported that death threats were made against Bissinger's life if he returned to Odessa.

News of the death threats were picked up by the media, and things went into a bit of an uproar. It was during this time that I was called in by the head football coach at Permian and told that the school superintendent had received a letter stating that I was involved in illegal recruiting practices. Specifically, the letter alleged that I was recruiting all the "good" black athletes in Odessa to play at Permian. The coach and I both knew this wasn't the case, and he dismissed the letter by saying he and the superintendent would not acknowledge letters written anonymously.

I never gave the letter a second thought at the time, mainly because it really didn't make any sense. I didn't *have* to recruit any of the black players to come to Permian. Permian was winning state championships and had a strong history and storied tradition of winning. People all across the state, and the nation, knew about MOJO.

Secondly, the black community knew me. I had coached in South Odessa for years. The parents knew that I cared and would do the right thing by their children. If they were coming to Permian, I didn't have to recruit them. They came simply because I coached there and they trusted me.

I thought I was done with it, but that would not be the case.

Not long after the anonymous letter was received, the entire coaching staff was called into a meeting with the head coach. He informed us that we were under investigation for violation of University Interscholastic League (UIL) rules. Reportedly, a secret videotape of our coaching staff was made. He figured it must have been made during the summer, and it was what the allegations were based upon. This video, which I never saw, started the snowball rolling downhill.

The video was turned over to the superintendent who, along with members of the School Board, determined we had indeed committed UIL rules infractions. The infractions dealt with grouping specific athletes for conditioning purposes during the summer months; the use of school facilities; and the actual participation of coaches. [2]

When the superintendent decided it would be a conflict of interest for him to make a ruling on the punishment for this infraction, the matter was passed to the UIL District Committee—made up of superintendents from our district—to decide the punishment phase of the infraction.

They determined that a violation had occurred, and reports hit newspapers all across the country. For days, the media played havoc with the story. My name and picture, as well as those of the other coaches, became common features in the local newspapers.

In the midst of this, the 1990-91 school year started and we began preparing for the football season. We had won the 1989 State Championship and had been named National Champions. When you combine that with the allegations of cheating, it made for a firestorm of controversy across the country.

As the story continued to unfold, I started receiving harassing messages every night on my answering machine. On several occasions, I noticed that I was being followed while driving. The perpetrators would drive so close, at times they almost touched the bumper on my car. When I would pull over to address them, they would speed off.

In the early stages of the investigation, every coach on the staff was named in the infraction. But somehow, coaches began to be eliminated from the list. When all was said and done, the list of alleged violators included only the head coach and three assistant coaches. My name was still at the top of the list, which piqued my interest. *How could all the others be removed from the list and my name still remain?* I really wanted to know how it was determined.

I asked the head coach for the details on the specific accusations. What was I accused of doing? In my mind, none of this fit. In the grand scheme of things, I didn't make decisions in regards to any issues involving the team.

When he said he didn't really know the specifics, I made an appointment to see the superintendent. It took two weeks for me to get a meeting.

During the meeting, I enquired as to what UIL rule was I being accused of violating. He explained that there was a UIL rule related to "grouping" athletes. It states that during the summer, coaches could watch players work out, but only from a distance of no less than 300 feet.

In July, the Permian coaching staff had made a visit to one of the junior high schools to watch the players work out. The superintendent explained that the video, which we later learned was provided by Jerry Taylor, the head football coach at Odessa High, showed that I was roughly twenty-three feet too close to the players—a distance less than the 300-feet limitation.

My name was plastered in newspapers from the East Coast to the West Coast. Even my own local papers reported that I was accused of cheating. I received harassing phone calls daily, and I continued to be followed. All of this the result of a video taken by a crosstown rival that showed me standing twenty-three feet too close to players while observing—not talking to—them.

Mr. Joe Rutledge, the vice principal at Permian at the time, called me into his office and asked how I was doing. I told him everything was going good.

Then, he asked another question: "Do you know why your name is in the middle of all of this?"

"No sir," I answered honestly.

I truly didn't know why anyone would write anonymous letters, make secret videotapes, or accuse me of violating UIL rules. I didn't feel I was important enough for anyone to do that. Why were these people after me?

"They want you out of the picture," Mr. Rutledge said. "Most of all, they feel you're the one that's holding these black kids together on this football team. They feel you're the one these players respect and listen to, and they are determined to get you. And a lot of it is originating from a few blacks in the community."

I respected and loved Mr. Rutledge and valued his opinions,

but this was hard for me to believe. I just couldn't see it.

As the days agonizingly turned into weeks, I remember receiving a series of phone calls one Saturday morning. My older sister and her husband called from California.

"Are you all right?" my sister asked. "You know your name is in the Los Angles paper for cheating?"

As soon as I finished talking to her, my sister-in-law called from Austin. Both she and my brother were on the phone, asking if I was OK.

"We just read your name in the morning paper for cheating," she said.

Shortly after that conversation, a friend called from Houston.

Same thing!

I'm sure if I had known someone in New York City, they would have called too. I couldn't believe this alleged infraction had made national headlines.

## The District Executive Committee

With the season well underway, we had to function in our roles as coaches while dealing with the fallout. Finally, we got the notice that a meeting with the UIL District Committee had been scheduled. Dressed in suits and ties, the four of us piled into a car and drove to Big Springs, Texas, where we thought our punishment would be decided.

The meeting didn't last long. The committee determined that the infractions were too large for them to decide the penalty, and chose instead to send us before the UIL State Committee in Austin, Texas. The hearing before that committee (if you can even call it a "hearing") was held in a ballroom at the Radisson Plaza Hotel in Austin. When we walked into the room, it was like a scene straight from the movies.

News reporters, photographers, and camera crews from all over the country filled the room. There was standing room only!

The UIL representatives included superintendents from all across the state of Texas. They were seated at a long table directly across from the four of us. Microphones had been placed at each chair.

I could tell by the looks on their faces they were primed and ready to pounce on us. It was a partisan committee—they wanted MOJO blood. Their whole intent and purpose was to be the axe that brought the Permian dynasty to its knees.

As I sat there taking in the surroundings, I bowed my head and prayed. The scales fell off my eyes as I prayed. Mr. Rutledge was right. This was a set up and I had been a marked target from the very beginning.

During my prayer it became clear that this was not about me, or Permian football, or rule violations, or the UIL State Committee. This was about my relationship with Jesus. In that moment, I made a vow to God and His Son, Jesus the Christ, that whatever happens: "Lord, when this is over I'm dedicating my life to serving You!"

When I opened my eyes, Bailey Marshall, director of the UIL, announced the penalty for the violations. The head coach was barred from participating in two games. Our team was ruled ineligible for playoffs, and the entire coaching staff at Permian was placed on probation for one year. We were told if we were involved in any future infractions that year, we would be banned from coaching in the state of Texas for life. At that time in the history of the UIL, no individual or school had been given a more severe punishment for a first-time violation.

Minutes from the committee meeting included the following statement, which further verified that the entire incident was (in my opinion and in the opinion of many others) a thinly disguised attempt to bring down the strength of Permian's football dominance:

"Marion Czaja moved and Alberto Byington seconded the motion to charge the ECISD with developing a plan by January 1, 1991, to dismantle the program that seems to have been in place for so many years ...³"

## Mike Wallace and *60 Minutes*

As if this wasn't enough distraction, TV journalist Mike Wallace and the crew from the TV news magazine, *60 Minutes*, added more rings to the already volatile circus when they arrived in Odessa to do an investigative piece. It was the most inopportune time, to say the least, as we were preparing to play our crosstown rival, Odessa High.

Odessa High had a great team, made up of great athletes. I know, because I had coached many of them in elementary and junior high school. They were undefeated for the season. We had confidence, even though we had lost to John Tyler the week before, because we had beaten Odessa High for twenty-eight straight years.

Mike Wallace and his crew were all over town conducting interviews. The only people off limits to them were the players and the coaching staff. The tension throughout the town created by the UIL's ruling, the book, and Wallace and his *60 Minutes* crew was thick enough to cut with a knife.

As the game approached, the tension grew ever thicker, and the hype created by Odessa High's success and our loss was driving sports fans crazy. The town buzzed with excitement. Sports analysts across the state were predicting this could be the year MOJO would fall.

The week's preparation for the game brought about an

amazing transformation in the players. The greater the tension, the more focused they became. On the day of the game, there was standing room only as 25,000 people showed up for the nationally televised match-up.

A photographer from California was allowed into our locker room to take pictures of our players. Afterward, he came out of the locker room and declared to the coaches that our players were amazingly focused. He said he had never seen kids behave like that. He said they were so focused you could hear a pin drop.

"I don't think they were even aware that I was in the room," he commented.

We won the game and it wasn't even close.

We ended the season with a record of 8-2, which was great for a Permian team that had been declared ineligible for the playoffs. The players had no championship motivation, but they prepared and played hard every week.

*If anyone really wanted to know the secret to the program's success, that was it—hard work and preparation. That's the MOJO mystic: Never, never, never give up—no matter what the circumstance.*

## A Vow to Keep

I was determined to keep the promise I made to the Lord during the hearing before the UIL state committee. When I say, "the scales fell," I mean that I realized God wanted to use this situation to draw me back to Him. I had gotten caught up in MOJO to such an extent that my relationship with Him had suffered. When I coached at the junior high level, I never missed a chance to be in church. My prayer life was strong. But, over time, I allowed my main focus to shift. It's hard not to get caught up when you have reached a celebrity-type status in a place. Frequently, people would buy my meals in a restaurant, or a police officer would let me go with a warning, when I deserved a ticket. I'd lost my way through it all. That is what God spoke to me during that hearing. That is what He showed me. And I was thankful for the opportunity He gave me to bring it all back to Him.

Fallout from the book and the UIL ruling would continue to affect the community, and the coaching staff. But I was committed to staying focused on developing my relationship with Jesus.

The trials and tribulations of that year had made me keenly aware of the meaning of true success. Those setbacks made me grateful, focused, and thankful for being tossed into the fire. The injustice I experienced, and the evil spoken about me, proved to be a huge advantage to my spiritual condition.

I knew if I stayed focused on God's Word and remained prayerful that He would do something amazing. My mother had a favorite verse from the Bible she'd quote. It's from John 15:7, where Jesus said, *"If you abide in me and my words abide in you, ask whatever you wish, and it will be done for you."* *(ESV)*

*I believe the things that were happening were of a spiritual nature. I knew that if I wanted to overcome the things others were doing then I had to focus on Jesus. It was not about them, or what they were doing or saying. It was about my personal walk with my Savior.*

Mr. Rutledge would become invaluable to me in those days, holding me accountable for my actions, mentoring me, and providing spiritual resources for me.

I remember finishing a workout at the local health club during the summer, just before the start of the '91 football season, when a gentleman approached me. I didn't know him, but I believed him to be a Permian supporter.

"Coach," he said, "how do you think the team is going to do this year?

I paused, knowing how I was feeling inside. Pent-up frustration and anger could have burst forward in that moment. But instead, I looked at him very calmly and said, "We won't stop until we're standing in the middle of Texas Stadium with our fingers in the air."

I could feel God was preparing to do something special with the team. The man smiled, shook my hand, and walked away.

During the 1991 season, Permian went a perfect 16-0 and we were again named the Texas State Champions. As we were traveling across the state winning all those games, I often wondered what the people on the UIL State and District Executive Committee, and Jerry Taylor were thinking about us. Did they recognize that even though they tried to bring us down, they didn't succeed?

## Hidden Agendas

Following that successful 1991 season, the opportunity presented itself for me to move from a coaching position at Permian High School into administration. I took the job. After the decision was announced, an elderly white gentleman approached me as I walked off the practice field one day. He looked like he was in his mid-sixties or early seventies. I had seen him on several occasions watching practice, but I didn't know his name.

He looked at me and asked, "You leaving?"

"Yes, sir," I told him.

"They won't win another one," he said, referring to the state championship. "You're the only coach out here these kids respect." I shook his hand, thanked him, and he walked off.

It was a humbling experience for me, even if it was just one person's opinion.

Shortly after, a school board member came to see me and asked if I had a moment to talk. We had walked out onto the practice field when he turned to me and said, "The night before the school board meeting, in which we would vote on the new teacher and administrative position for the district, I got a call from a lady who asked me not to vote for you to be a principal at Permian. She said the reason she was asking me not to vote for you was because of your temper. She cited the incident where you got upset during the game against Midland Lee, and had to be restrained by the coaches.

He told me this woman had called each board member to ask that they not consider me for the position.

"Obviously, we didn't take her seriously, because you got the job," the man told me. "I think the reason she did it was to keep you coaching at Permian. That's the only thing that makes any sense. I thought you needed to know."

We shook hands, and I thanked him. I had no idea who this lady was, or why she would be interested in whether I was a coach or a principal. Three years later, and here I was again in a situation where someone had tried to control my future. I wasn't any different from any of the other coaches on our staff. I didn't want to remain an assistant coach for the rest of my life. I wanted options, and I wasn't getting any younger. Once again, I knew that God had a purpose and a plan for this adversity. I just needed to wait for the blessing that would come out of it.

I had another peek into the hidden agendas of others when

Ricky Williams, a close friend of mine who had taught at Odessa High during the time I coached and taught at Permian, had invited me to visit him in Carlsbad, New Mexico, where he had moved and was coaching high school football.

When I arrived to watch one of his scrimmages, Ricky was standing outside the field house talking to a former black assistant football coach from Odessa High. I remembered him as one of the coaches on staff at the same time I was coaching at Permian.

I had no animosity toward any of the coaches at Odessa High because they were simply following orders in their attempts to bring us down. When I walked up, Ricky said they had just been discussing me. I shook Ricky's hand, then greeted the other coach. Then Ricky looked at me and said, "Listen to this."

The former Odessa High coach said to me: "We knew we had to get you. We knew you were the one controlling those black athletes at Permian. When we found out that you had moved to administration, and wasn't on the sidelines with the team any more, we got excited. Now, we knew we had a chance to beat you."

As I listened to what the coach was saying, I knew he was telling me the truth. Mr. Rutledge had said the same thing to me. It wasn't about being twenty feet too close, specific grouping, or the use of school facilities. It was about those "good" black athletes I was accused of recruiting and Odessa High losing to Permian for twenty-eight straight years. I believed it was the reason Jerry Taylor wanted to keep my name in the middle of the UIL rules violation. His comment that it was common knowledge in the black community regarding my recruitment of players was the basis for his action.

I believe it was also the motive behind the letter to the superintendents in Odessa, Midland, Abilene, and San Angelo, and the School Board. They all knew the real reason. I was the one in the dark. But God always has a way of bringing dark things to the light. Our God is all about revealing the truth. And it comes in some of the most unexpected ways.

I was named Outstanding Principal of the year for Region 18 by the Texas Association of Secondary School Principals at the end of my second year in administration. At the end of my third year, I resigned and enrolled in seminary at Southern Methodist University's Perkins School of Theology. God had been faithful to me, and I wanted to keep my promise to Him.

The trials, setbacks, and disappointments I endured that year, of which I've only presented a small portion here, helped me define the God-driven, God-ordained purpose for my life. The calling was clear. The more adversity I endured, the clearer God's plan for my life became. This had been a test of my faith.

## A Serious Disservice

When I looked back on the things that took place at Permian during that 1990 season, I see it as a serious disservice to the students in the community. During the turmoil with the UIL rules infractions, the Permian coaching staff had to give depositions to the school attorney. After giving my deposition, in which I answered a series of questions, the attorney concluded by asking was there anything else I would like to add.

I had much to say, but I settled with telling him: "I think the people who are doing this, the people who are trying to destroy this football team, are making a serious mistake. I do not believe they understand the implications of their actions. They're not just destroying the football team, they're destroying kids' lives—innocent kids who had nothing to do with any of this.

"Why can't we have two great teams in the city, and promote

that?"

A portrait of what I was referring to was framed for me years later after I had moved away from Odessa and came back for a speaking engagement. I had been shopping in Dunlap's, a local department store in Odessa, when I walked up to the counter to pay for my items. There was a young lady working behind the counter that day, who looked to be high school aged, or maybe a freshman in college.

As she checked me out at the register, she inquired about the 1989 National Championship ring I was wearing, and asked if I played football at Permian. When I told her I had coached football at Permian for a number of years, she responded by saying, "I'm a senior at Permian and we have nothing like that."

I was deeply affected by her words. I could see the disappointment in her eyes when she made the statement. I knew what she meant. Permian was now losing games—even to Odessa High. There was no excitement, no glory in the MOJO name anymore. No talk of winning state championships. The students had nothing to look forward to.

All the coaches I worked with at Permian during the glory years were gone. We were scattered all over the state. I believe with all my heart if that coaching staff were still there, Permian would still be winning state championships. There's no doubt in my mind about that.

The School Board had brought in another coach, who literally wanted to destroy the tradition. I was told he went as far as taking down the pictures of the previous teams and players' accomplishments from the wall and throwing them in the trash.

When the Permian football team was operating at its apex, it produced almost a half million dollars in revenue each year for the school district. During those state championship years, hundreds of students at the school were involved—from the band, to the cheerleaders, to the pep squads.

Thousands from the community got involved as well in various capacities, not to mention the strong support of parents in the Booster Club. It was reported the mobile home caravan following the team around the state was twenty-three miles long. It was amazing to have community involvement of that magnitude.

Students who were not involved in any extracurricular activities also benefited from the team's success just by coming to the games and taking part in the pep rallies and other school activities. Just walking around in a Permian letter jacket or tee shirt generated a source of pride.

It gave everyone a sense of belonging to something special.

That's what the young lady in Dunlap's was saying that day. It's also what I was saying to the attorney, following my deposition. The lives of all those innocent students were affected by people who had an agenda.

Leaders must know how to place their personal agendas aside for the good of others. That doesn't mean leaders roll over when it comes to matters of right and wrong. Leaders do need to know when to stand up for what's right, but in this situation, there was no search for justice. It was a witch hunt fueled by envy. A good leader can discern a hidden agenda from a true pursuit of justice. If you have any confusion, your grounding in God's Word will guide you. If your pursuit aligns with God's Word, you are on a good path. If it does not, then you better step off and give yourself a check.

# PART 2:
# My Early Stories

*Above: A young Nate Hearne in front of their 3-room house with his brother and the family dog.*

*To the right: Nate wearing his Sunday best clothing, as he poses with his aunt and cousin.*

# Chapter 5
# We All Have a Story

*"On a day with enough words and rhetoric to fill a year's worth of meetings, picture of silence summed up the fate of the Permian football program. After all but the last reporters, committee members and coaches had filed out of the eighth floor of the Radisson Plaza Hotel, Panther assistant Nate Hearne sat motionless on a window sill, draped by the downtown skyline."*

-*Odessa American*, September 21, 1990
editorial by Garry Leavell[1]

I grew up in Andrews, Texas; a small, oil-producing, West-Texas community. In the 1950s through 1970s, when I was there, Andrews had a population of somewhere between 8,000 and 10,000. Our community was deeply segregated.

For example, blacks (or coloreds as we were referred to) were not allowed to enter through the front door of a restaurant. We had to go around to a marked back door. The local movie theaters made blacks sit in the balcony. The schools were segregated as well.

I came from what would be considered a rather large family. I had seven siblings; five girls and two boys (a ninth child, a boy, died at birth). I was the fourth oldest.

We lived in a small frame, three-room house. Not a three-bedroom house, but a three-*room* house that rested on cinder blocks. We had no hot water, and the bathroom, which was known as an "outhouse," was literally outside the house. We used the stove to heat water for washing and bathing, and we took our baths in a No. 3 foot tub.

My parents were products of the 1930s, and knew what it was like to live within the restrictions of the Jim Crow segregation laws. Though they've probably heard a bit about the days of slavery, young people growing up today probably know nothing about Jim Crow laws, which, in my opinion, did as much to hurt the black race as slavery.

My mother completed the tenth grade. She was the spiritual head of our family, and even had the keys to the church. When the preacher didn't show up, she would conduct the worship service. She was always cooking meals for the sick, cleaning the church, and ministering to people in the community. She met and married my father when she was sixteen years old. During most of our childhood, she worked as a "domestic," meaning she cleaned other people's houses—mostly the wealthy whites in the community—for a living.

I can still remember some of the stories she would tell us about the abuse and prejudice she endured working for white families back in those days. But like most black women during those times, she withstood whatever abuse she was given without resistance because she knew she had to provide for her family. One of the good things to come out of those days was the fact that sometimes the people my mother worked for would give her their children's used or hand-me-down clothes to bring home to me and my siblings. I remember in elementary school having only three pairs of blue jeans, and each pair had holes in them. I had three "good" shirts that I switched up. They also had holes.

There was no school bus service provided to my school, so we had to walk to school—even in bad weather. I recall several occasions where I had to put cardboard in my shoes to protect my feet from the elements, because the soles of my shoes were so worn. I used the cardboard to keep the heat out in the summer, the water out when it rained, and the cold out in the winter. Most of the food we ate was given to us through government subsidized food programs.

My father was the sixth child in a family of thirteen children. He was the son of a sharecropper from Arkansas, and he quit school in the third grade. He worked at a full-service Humble (which later became Exxon) gas station.

What I remember most about my father was the instinct he displayed for teaching critical life lessons at the appropriate time. He was a strong disciplinarian, a man of few words, a visionary, and very confident in his abilities. He never learned to read or write, but he had a photographic memory. If he saw something once, he would never forget it.

## My First Role Model

Although my parents were always there for us, and had a major influence on our lives, it's probably fair to say the title of "role model" in my life would easily have been given to my older sister, Evelyn.

She was responsible for our care when our parents were working. In the absence of our parents, Evelyn ruled lovingly, but with an iron glove. She mastered it well. This was a difficult task for her, but she never quit or complained.

Evelyn was eleven years old when she was given the full responsibility of running the house and caring for her four younger siblings—ranging in age from one to eight years old. She had to grow up fast, because taking care of us was a real challenge. Growing up in poverty was difficult enough, but growing up in poverty and having to provide for younger siblings added a whole new dynamic to the problem.

Evelyn was intelligent, diligent, and disciplined. She had to be, considering we were always hungry, adventurous, and creative. I mean, we were creative in the sense of finding ways to get into trouble—something we all did really well.

She nurtured, affirmed, and cared for us. She washed and ironed our clothes, she cooked our meals, she helped us with our homework and, when it was time to discipline us, she did it with a maturity exceeding her age. When our parents were away, we were loyal to her to a fault. Because of her sacrifice, we developed a deep love and admiration for her. The one thing we all knew about our sister, Evelyn, was that she loved us unconditionally.

When the public school system integrated in Andrews, Texas, Evelyn was a straight-A student at the all-black school. She entered Andrews High School as a sophomore and continued to make straight As. She graduated as a member of the National Honor Society, and earned the right to be recognized as the salutatorian. But the administration from the school district would not allow it. They made a decision to not count her ninth grade scores. The administration declared that because Evelyn had attended the all-black school her ninth-grade year, her grades would be considered unacceptable at the all-white school.

Evelyn's English teacher didn't think the decision was a fair one, and came to our home to discuss it with my parents. She suggested my parents take the matter before the school's administration. Not understanding how the system worked, I believe my mother and father were a little intimidated by the process. Instead of fighting the decision, they told Evelyn's teacher they were happy that she was making good grades. They thanked her for letting them know and it was not mentioned again.

After graduating, Evelyn really didn't know what she was going to do. But two white ladies in the community encouraged her to go to college and pursue nursing. One of the women was a nurse whose house my sister had cleaned for several years. The other woman was the wife of the man who owned the Humble Service Station where my father worked. They, too, had known our family for many years.

Both women admired Evelyn, constantly told her how smart she was, and encouraged her to go to college. It inspired Evelyn that two white women were encouraging her, a black woman, to go to school and pursue her dreams. No one at the high school, other than her English teacher, had ever mentioned anything to her about pursuing a college education.

When it was clear that my parents could not afford to send her to school, these two women offered to pay for Evelyn to attend the local community college, and provide her with transportation.

She enrolled in the nursing program at Odessa College, graduated cum laude, and went to work as a registered nurse in the emergency room at the local hospital in Andrews, Texas. For the next ten years, she lived with us and used her salary to help my parents with expenses. Even after graduating from college, Evelyn remained in that "motherly" mode, doing things like helping us with homework, buying us clothes and school supplies, and making sure we always had lunch money.

She also provided transportation to and from school for us. We are, and always will be, indebted to our sister, Evelyn, because of her sacrifice—for giving up her life for family. What she did for us is beyond the comprehension of many people in our society today. The message kids often hear is, "You've got to look out for yourself, because if you don't, no one else will."

Kids today don't need to be tossed out on their own to see if they can make it. They need leaders who will show them that someone cares for them. Kids need examples, like Evelyn's, that show them that there are people willing to sacrifice their own comfort to help them succeed.

*Evelyn was a tangible example to me of the agape love that Jesus has for each of us. Agape love is a self-sacrificing, unconditional love that declares, "I am on your side, no matter what the cost."*

If a leader is prepared to give that kind of love to those in his or her influence, he or she will automatically be pointing others to Jesus.

The love, respect, and admiration we hold in our hearts for Evelyn grows deeper each year. The character she displayed during those years produced a depth of loyalty in each of us so that, to this day, when she calls out our names: "Rayfield, Mittie, Nathanial, Gloria, Jackie, Kenneth, and Debbie!" we line up in obedience like ducklings.

# Chapter 6
# An Unwelcome Integration

---

*"As a result of this desegregation, football became the one arena in town where blacks could be sure to gain acceptance. 'We don't have to deal with blacks here,' said Lanita Akins, a devout Permian fan who was active in county Democratic Party politics. 'We don't have any contact with them, except on the Permian football team. It's the only place in Odessa where people interact at all with blacks.'"*
-*Friday Night Lights* by H.G. Bissinger[1]

---

My first taste of public school was at the Lincoln School in Andrews, Texas. Lincoln was a school for kids in grades one through twelve that was established in 1950 to provide education for black children. I went there through third grade, and for the most part, those first years of school were exciting to me.

I didn't have the same fears and concerns that many kids have when they leave home and family for the first time to begin a new stage in life among total strangers. That's because during those early years, my two sisters, my brother, and I were very close, and we attended the same school.

It made school an extension of my home life. My sisters and brother watched over me and made sure I was safe, but they also doled out reprimands when they saw me doing something wrong.

We lived within walking distance of the schoolhouse, so my friends and I played often and had fun going to and from school. Every day was an adventure—filled with laughter, play, and exploration. From a financial standpoint, we were all pretty much on the same level. No one was financially better off than anyone else. We all had patches on our jeans, holes in our socks, and hand-me-down, run-over shoes.

The same story line pretty much ran through every family. The interesting thing, though, was that we never knew we were poor. That is, until the school district closed our school and we were forced to attend the white school as part of integration.

I remember my mother telling me when the integration was announced that Lincoln was no longer an option, and that I might as well get used to it because I would be going to school with white children.

I told her I didn't want to go, and even refused to leave the house that first morning with my sisters and brother. Telling my mother what I would not do was always a bad idea. My mother didn't buy into my resistance, and she made it perfectly clear that day that she was serious about us receiving an education.

Looking back, I really had no reason not to want to go to a white school. I had limited interactions with white kids, so there was nothing there to suggest my experience would be a bad one. Besides, my sisters and brother would be there too, just as they had been at Lincoln.

I just didn't want to go. All my friends were black (not that I ever really paid that any attention), and I had come to know them very well. I didn't like the thought of not having my old school, or not being with my same friends. Those new, white kids would be total strangers.

## A Harsh Dose of Reality

If I didn't have a reason for not wanting to go to the new school on the morning of the first day, I certainly had one by the time the day ended. In one single day, all my fears and concerns were affirmed.

My first day of school, I learned that I smelled bad, that I was ugly, that I was poor, and that I was black. My teachers didn't like me. When my teachers handed things to me, they let go of them in such a way that they fell onto the floor. None of my classmates would even talk to me or play with me.

For all practical purposes, I was an outcast. And this was only the first day of school! It was the opposite of what I had been used to at Lincoln. I was devastated. I wasn't welcome there, and when I left school that day, I was determined to never go back.

Of course, that attitude didn't get me very far with my mother. The next day, I was right back in school—forced to mingle and learn among a group of people who treated me worse than dirt. There were three difficult situations from that time that continue to stand out in my mind.

## It's My Lunch

One of the most humiliating moments for me—one I'm likely to never forget—happened when I was in fifth grade. My family didn't have much money, so my parents couldn't afford to give the four of us lunch money for school each day. Instead, my mother would pack us each a bologna sandwich (made only with meat and bread—no mayonnaise, lettuce, tomatoes, or cheese), and give us each two cents to buy a carton of milk.

If you know anything about Texas, you know that we endure some of the strangest weather in the country. The winters are short with very little snow (if we have any at all), and temperatures can reach into the triple digits in the summer.

In the 1950s and 1960s, school buildings didn't have air conditioning, so you can imagine what it was like in the classrooms when temperatures began to soar. You might also imagine what heat like that does to lunch meat over a period of time.

Our lockers were located inside the classroom, where we stored our personal belongings—including schoolbooks, coats, and our lunches. One day, as the teacher was going over a lesson, one of my classmates told the teacher there was something that smelled in the locker next to her desk. The teacher asked whose locker it was. I raised my hand.

"What's in it?" she asked.

"My lunch," I responded.

"When did you put it in there?"

I told her I had just put my lunch in there that morning, but my classmates said, "No, it's been in there all week."

The teacher didn't ask me any questions, she just said, "Throw it away!"

It was my lunch for the day. If I threw it away, then I'd have nothing to eat the whole day. And there was a strong possibility there wouldn't be much at home after school. It would have been hard to make it through the day on a carton of milk.

Embarrassed, I removed the lunch bag from my locker and took it outside. Only, I didn't throw it away as my teacher had instructed. Instead, I decided to eat the sandwich. When I returned to class, my teacher asked what I did with the sandwich. When I told her I ate it, she ordered me to go to the principal's office. The principal never ask me what happened, he just gave me three licks for disobeying my teacher.

**The Pushup**

One day during my gym class, the teacher asked me to demonstrate to the other students the proper way to do pushups. He was upset because the white students in class were not doing the pushups to his satisfaction. In hindsight, I think he took stock in that old stereotypical view that blacks were more athletically gifted than whites. I was the only black student in the class.

At first, I was hesitant to "perform" before him and the others. But then I reasoned that this could be my moment—that by showing I was talented at something, I would get the attention and earn the respect of my fellow classmates for doing something good. I thought maybe it would be my moment of glory.

That thought was short-lived, however, when the teacher looked at me and, in front of the class filled with white students, said: "OK Smokey, show them how to do a proper pushup."

Just as quickly as my pride had swollen at the opportunity to impress those around me, I was deflated by those damning words. My moment of glory had been reduced to a few seconds of embarrassment, prompted by a racial slur. The whole class laughed and snickered at me. *What did he call me?* I thought. My name wasn't Smokey, and he knew it.

I don't know if he thought about the fact that he was insulting me, and that his motive was to embarrass me in front of the class. That kind of language was fairly common in those days coming from whites. But as a 9-year-old kid, I just knew I was being laughed at.

I chose not to allow the teacher the privilege of reducing me to the status of a circus animal putting on a show, and I refused to do the pushup. Instead, I just sat there. When he asked me again to perform, still referring to me as Smokey, I just sat there in silence, with the whole class intently watching the both of us. When he realized I was not going to do as he had asked, the teacher moved on to the next exercise, and I sat out the rest of the class.

**I Do Not Allow ...**

There is one other painful experience I remember from that time of my life that I want to share. It is one that started out with promise. Somehow, despite our family's financial situation, my parents allowed me to join the Cub Scouts and actually came up with the money to buy my uniform.

That was monumental in my life, because it gave me the chance to be a part of something positive and special in our community. It also provided me an extra set of clothes to wear to school—one that wasn't worn or had patches on the knees and elbows.

I also was able to try out for the Little League baseball team in our community, and I was selected by the Cubs. Our games were played during the week, and the baseball field was within walking distance from the school. One day, we had a baseball game scheduled after school.

I changed out of my Cub Scouts uniform into my baseball uniform and was walking out of the school building when someone called to me. Turning to see who it was, I recognized the person as one of my classmates. He also played baseball, but for another team—the Giants.

I was surprised to hear him call my name. Although we were in the same class, he had never spoken to me before that day. He asked if I was headed to the ballpark. When I said yes, he asked if he could walk along with me.

Surprised at his request, I said that would be fine. Then, he said he needed to stop by his house first to change into his baseball uniform. He asked if I would come with him. I agreed.

When we reached his home, he stopped short of walking up to his house and said he would have to ask his mother if I could come inside. I waited in the driveway as he walked up to the front door and knocked.

When his mother appeared at the front door, he asked her if I could come inside, and then I heard his mother say, "You know I don't allow those filthy niggers in my house!"

I turned and left.

Later, at the ballpark, he said to me, "I'm sorry for what my mother said."

I didn't reply. That wasn't the first time I had experienced racism like that.

These three experiences made a big impact on me during an impressionable time in my life. I later discovered it was in these perceived disadvantaging situations I learned how truly advantageous they were to my future success.

It took me a while to see the advantages. My experiences at the school potentially caused me to label myself a failure. And, for a while, that appeared to be the case. Elementary school, for me, was a disaster. I left there with very low self-esteem.

My report cards were a reflection of that low self-esteem. I never made a grade higher than a C in class. I got lots of Ds and Fs. Those were very difficult days for me and I told my mother on the last day of grade school, that I was never going back. If elementary school was that bad, I reasoned that junior high would only be worse.

## Turn Around

My mother wasn't interested in hearing what I wanted. She knew what was best for me, and staying away from school was definitely *not* in my best interest. Not only that, it was against the law.

I expected junior high to be even worse than elementary

school, and the start of the first day went exactly how I figured it would. When I walked into my first period English class, I was virtually ignored by the teacher.

I made my way to a desk at the back of the classroom. Being in the back of the class, I reasoned, would make me less likely to be called on, and I would not have to worry about my classmates picking at me behind my back.

That was my strategy of survival for each of my classes that day. And it looked like it was going to work—until I entered my fifth period science class and encountered the teacher, Mr. Clyde Haak.

Standing in the doorway, I looked for my favorite seat—in the corner, in the back, in the dark. It was then that Mr. Haak looked up and saw me.

"You must be Nathan," he said. "I've heard a lot of wonderful things about you."

I wasn't sure he was talking to me; no teacher had ever told me they had heard wonderful things about me. So I turned to look behind me to see if some one else was standing there. There was no one else. Mr. Haak walked up, shook my hand, and put his arm around my back. He guided me to a seat at the front of the class. This was all new to me, a teacher treating me like this!

"Nathan, you and I are going to have a wonderful time in this science class. I have arranged seating, and this is your desk." He pointed to a desk in the front row, directly in front of his desk. At that point, I knew I was in trouble, because I had never been a front-row student.

That was about to change, and Mr. Haak would play a big part in the change. Mr. Haak specialized in character development, and somehow, someone had told him about me. He had taken me on as a project for success. Every day I had a special encounter in

Mr. Haak's class.

When he spoke to the class, it was as though he was speaking directly to me. He smiled often, and when he did speak to me, he would look me in the eyes. Mr. Haak always greeted me with a smile, a handshake, and a word of encouragement. Just being in his presence and being a part of his class made me feel special.

My last class of the day was seventh grade football. Mark Wallace, a rugged bear of a man who stood 6'4" and spoke in a deep, gruff voice, was the coach. Standing in line outside the field house along with the other seventh graders who had signed up for football, I watched as Coach Wallace walked in my direction.

Extending his hand to me, he said, "You must be Hearne. I've heard a lot of wonderful things about you. You're going to be on my team and we're going to have a lot of fun winning football games."

I went home that first day of school walking on a cloud. I couldn't wait for the next day so I could return to school. In fact, I was so excited I left home without my lunch. My mom thought I was insane—one day I hated school and the next day I loved it.

Why the change? It was because I had been affirmed. As a young black student in a predominately all-white school, that's what I needed more than anything else. I'd been so beaten up and ridiculed my first few years in school that I never thought anyone would say something nice to me, and certainly not show me the kindness I was receiving from these two men.

Mr. Haak and Coach Wallace had a plan and they implemented it to perfection. They showed me a kind of love and respect that made me feel I was worth something, that I could learn, and that I could achieve great things. And, I believed in them. They believed in me, and I didn't want to let them down.

The next few weeks in class, and on the football field, proved to be the most memorable and rewarding days of my life—and actually marked the turning point for me.

In Mr. Haak's class, for instance, I began to get involved in learning—even raising my hand to answer questions. I remember the first time I raised my hand to answer a question. I could tell Mr. Haak was excited to see it. His reaction made me want to answer another question.

On Saturday morning of that week, I played one of those football games that one remembers the rest of his life. Under Coach Wallace's instruction, and with him encouraging me all the way, I rushed for 280 yards, scored four touchdowns, and intercepted a pass on defense.

It was a game where I emerged as the star, and it was all because of Coach Wallace. He encouraged me, he affirmed me, and he supported me. He felt that I could do it, and he encouraged me to believe in myself as well. At the end of the game, Coach Wallace gave me a big bear hug and said, "Hearne, that was just outstanding!"

His wife even came up and gave me a hug. She told me that I was wonderful. She was a beautiful lady. No female teacher at my elementary school had ever hugged me and told me I was wonderful. It was a special feeling.

The following Monday, something even more terrific happened for me in Mr. Haak's science class. It was the end of the first six weeks of school and after checking the attendance, Mr. Haak walked by and laid my report card on my desk, face down. When I turned it over, I saw that I had received an A in science. It was the very first A I made in public school.

When he finished passing out the report cards, Mr. Haak said, "Boys and girls, I need your attention." Then, he looked at me and said, "Nathan, stand up."

First, he told the class about my performance during Saturday's football game, which came as a surprise because I didn't even know he was there.

Then, Mr. Haak said: "Class, Nathan is not only an outstanding athlete, but he's also an A student in this class. And for his outstanding efforts, I'm going to make him my lab assistant."

I had no clue what a lab assistant was, but as I stood there with all my classmate's eyes on me, Mr. Haak walked to the back of the room and opened up the closet. He removed a white folded bundle. He unfolded the bundle and presented me with a brand-new white lab coat.

The classmate who sat next to me kept looking at the pocket on the coat. When I looked down, I saw that Mr. Haak had written my name on the pocket. In that moment, my whole life changed.

I share these positive experiences with you because I truly believe this is what our children need today. Nurturing, affirming, and building character are at the heart of what this book is about.

*The affirmation I received in Mr. Haak's seventh grade science class, and the support and encouragement shown me on the football field by Coach Wallace, literally changed my life forever.*

I went from being a student of low self-esteem, who made Cs, Ds, and Fs on all his report cards in elementary school, to making As and Bs not just in Mr. Haak's science class, but in all my classes. I went from being a student who wanted to drop out of school, to being a student whose number one desire was to become a science teacher and a football coach.

What Mr. Haak and Coach Wallace did for me was all about

character development. They not only repeatedly told me that I wasn't defined by the clothes I wore or the bologna sandwiches I brought to school for lunch, but they showed me that making Ds and Fs were not an indicator of my intelligence. Helping me shape my character helped me improve my grades. The advantage of disadvantages changed my life.

## The Advantage

It would be foolish to assume that my earlier problems were only because I was a black student in the white school. Judgment and prejudice happens everywhere. When I attended Lincoln, my first through third grade teacher was a tall, light-skinned, black woman.

She treated the light-skinned black students in the classroom with a partiality that she didn't show the others. She would give them special treats and extra play time. I don't remember her ever doing anything special for me. But I do remember her giving me licks and saying hateful things to me.

There was a short, light-skinned black teacher at the school who was always nice to me. She would smile and give me things, even though she wasn't my teacher.

When we integrated in the 60s in Andrews, I remember feeling that my teachers and the principal cared nothing for me. My teachers at the elementary school never spoke a positive word to me. They seemed to take delight in embarrassing me at every opportunity.

When I left elementary and began junior high school, I received the total opposite treatment from Mr. Haak and Coach Wallace, who were both white. They were very affirming. As I continued my formative education, I encountered more of these kinds of behavioral extremes.

Thinking it was an advantage to attend an all-black school with black teachers was not true. Thinking it was a disadvantage to attend an all-white school with white teachers was also not true.

The important lesson I learned was to judge people by the content of their character. I continued to encounter these experiences throughout my formal education in Andrews. While one white teacher would hate me, another white teacher would help me.

I remember an incident during my senior year in high school. My English teacher had given us time to put things away and get ready for the next class. As we waited for the bell to ring, one student in class asked the teacher what she did to have fun when she was a child. The teacher thought for a second and said she and her friends would gather up chinaberries, put them in a "nigger shooter," and shoot them at each other.

After she said it, she looked at me. Another student and I were the only blacks in the class. I walked out of the class and decided that I would not go back. The principal tried to apologize for the teacher's behavior, but I had my mind made up that I wasn't going back into the class. That story made its way around the faculty quickly. The next day as I was sitting in the foyer area, a teacher I had during my freshman year walked up and sat next to me. She was young, and I remember her being very tall with short brown hair.

She said she heard about what had happened in my English class and that she was so very sorry. Then, she began to weep. As she sat there holding my hand and crying, I knew without a doubt her feelings for me were sincere.

I believe when Dr. Martin Luther King said one day he hoped his children would be judged by the content of their character and not the color of their skin, he was speaking for every ethnicity. I've seen blacks do everything they could to destroy me, and I've met blacks who have done everything they could to help me. I've found that to be true in every race.

I've found that people, whatever their nationality or background, who are willing to help and not judge, are people of character. Their character was developed and nurtured by parents or some other significant figure in their lives. There's also a spiritual connotation to it. They know Jesus and have developed a relationship with Him. The environment we live in molds our character traits.

Learning this concept at a very early age was a tremendous asset for me. I have displayed that spirit in the classroom, during my coaching, as an administrator, and as a pastor. Students, parents, teachers, and congregants of every ethnicity have seen it in me; they respond to it, and affirm it. It's God's calling on my life.

## Desire to Go to College

During my junior year in high school, I made the varsity basketball team. Coach Edd Farmer was the coach at that time. The last game of the season, four seniors on the team fouled out. Coach Farmer placed me in the game. We were ahead 82-80, with seconds on the clock. I took the ball, drove the lane, made the shot, was fouled, and I made the free throw. We won the game 85-80.

Coach Farmer was complimentary after the game. As my junior year came to a close, I had high hopes for my senior year. I knew he liked me and he would give me an opportunity to play, increasing my chances to get a college scholarship. I was too slow to make it in football and I knew my best shot was to make it in basketball, especially because I was playing strong. But that was not to be. Coach Farmer left the school after my junior year and was replaced with a new coach. Then, I had a freak accident during practice one day. I slipped and fell, and all my weight landed on my thumb. I had to sit out for five weeks. I worked extremely hard to make it back into the line-up, but the new coach had a different plan.

Midway through the season, the new coach called me into his office and told me I had a bad attitude. He said I acted like I thought I knew it all, and that I was uppity. In short, he said he didn't need me anymore and dismissed me from the team. I didn't see myself as being any of those things he said about me. I cried. It was so embarrassing, and I saw all my hopes of going to college swirling down the drain.

Despite being dismissed from the team, I was determined to show him all those negative things he said about me were not true. I set my heart to prove him wrong.

On May 25, 1970, I graduated from high school. I remember it vividly because it was a pivotal moment in my life. My mother came to my graduation. I remember receiving my diploma and wading through the crowd after the ceremony to find her.

She hugged and kissed me, and told me how proud she was of me. Then, she held me at arm's length with tears in her eyes and said, "You need to go see your father. He wants to talk to you."

I made a beeline to the Humble Service Station on Main Street where my father worked. When I arrived, he was in the office. I walked in, and he motioned to a chair. I sat.

I didn't know what to expect next.

"I told your mother to tell you I wanted to talk to you because you needed to hear this from me," my father began. "I know you want to go to school, but I have nothing for you—no money, and no transportation. I have too many mouths left at that house to feed."

Then he leaned forward in his chair and gave me a look we

all knew meant serious business, and said, "But I want you to be somebody. I want you to make something out of yourself. I don't want to see you on the streets. I don't want to hear about you being on drugs, and I don't want to hear that you've been locked up in somebody's jail. I want you to be somebody, and make something out of yourself."

Sitting there looking in my father's eyes, with his words ringing in my ears, I knew that, at age seventeen, I was on my own. If I was going to go to college I had better find a way to make it happen.

I got a job working as a sacker and a stocker at Piggly Wiggly Supermarket on Main Street in Andrews, Texas. I worked that job the entire summer, bagging groceries from 7 o'clock in the morning until 5 p.m. each day, six days a week. On Mondays, Wednesdays, and Fridays, I would arrive at 4 a.m., unload semi-trucks until 6 a.m., then go home, change clothes, and report back to work at 7 a.m. I saved every penny I made, which amounted to $250—enough to cover my college tuition.

I know that doesn't sound like a lot of money by today's standards, but this was the early 1970s, when minimum wage was $1.35 an hour. In 1970, you could buy a gallon of gasoline for 25 cents. During that time, a Whataburger with fries and a large drink was only $1.30, and a brand new pair of Levis jeans, without the holes in them, only cost $5.

The $250 I saved was enough for me to enroll in the Junior College.

My older brother, who was serving in the U.S. Marine Corp., was fighting in the Vietnam War at the time. He was a squadron leader on recon in the jungle. But he took a moment that summer to write home, which proved to be a big encouragement to me. In his letter, he said he had heard about my disappointing senior year and encouraged me not to give up. He also told me that the head basketball coach at Odessa College awarded three scholarships each year to walk-ons.

"I've seen you play," he wrote, "and you play well enough to get one of those scholarships. Don't give up on your dream."

My brother was my hero, and I didn't want to disappoint him. His words meant a lot to me. If I truly wanted to get a scholarship, I would have to work at it. And I did just that. Every day after work, I would practice my basketball skills and play pick-up games with friends from the neighborhood. We didn't have an indoor gym available, so we played and practiced on an outdoor black top. The weather never stopped us from playing. We practiced in the rain, the heat, and even during those West Texas dust storms. By the time summer ended, I could do just about anything I wanted to do with a basketball.

As summer ended, one day I was walking through the kitchen while my mother was cooking. She stopped me.

"I know your father told you he didn't have anything for you to go to school, and that he didn't have any transportation," she said. "But there's a Greyhound bus that comes through here every morning at 5 a.m. You can catch that bus and it will drop you off in front of that school in the mornings, and come back through there at 6 p.m. and pick you up. You can ride that bus until you make your way."

By saying "make your way," she meant until I could get a scholarship.

On Monday, the day I was to report to school, my mother woke me up at 4 o'clock in the morning. She had breakfast already prepared for me. After breakfast, she took me to the bus station. She hugged and kissed me, and told me she was proud of me. There was one thing I knew for sure about my mother—she would be praying for me. That was a huge plus. We all knew her prayers worked.

Odessa College was thirty miles from my hometown. I rode the bus, engulfed in deep thought and complete silence, wondering how things would turn out, and would I be able to get a scholarship to attend college?

The bus driver pulled up in front of the college, released the air breaks and swung open those double doors. I stepped off the bus with my workout gear in a sack. My workout gear was a tank top, a pair of hot pants that we called workout shorts in those days, and two pairs of the white tube socks that came up to my knees. My Chuck Taylors were tied together by the strings and thrown over my shoulder.

I wore a large Afro back in those days.

I had my $250 in my front pocket, held together with a rubber band. I read the signs and made my way to registration, paid my tuition then bought my books, notebook paper, and pens. Surprisingly, I had some change left over.

My next move was to find the gym. I asked some people for help and they pointed me in the right direction. I walked up to the gym door and there was a sign that read: "Tryouts starting today in the main gym at 2 p.m. If interested, sign up in coaches' office." It was signed, "Coach L.M. McCullough."

When I walked into the office, Coach Mac (I later learned that was how he preferred to be addressed) was seated behind his desk. He had a slim build, with greying temples. Even though he was seated, I guessed him to be about 6' 5". He wore a white polo shirt with "Odessa College Wranglers" emblazoned on the pocket, long white khaki pants with a white belt, and size 15 Chuck Taylors.

He was, in the terminology of today's youth, "old school,"

from top to bottom.

Coach Mac had been the head coach at Odessa College for twenty-five years.

"Are you here to try out for the team?" he asked, looking up at me.

"Yes, sir," I answered.

Coach Mac explained that tryouts would start at 2 o'clock that day, and continue through Friday. He said he would announce who would be receiving the three scholarships on Friday.

"Are you still interested?" he asked.

"Yes, sir."

He handed me a clipboard so that I could sign-up. I thanked him and then left his office to find my first class. My routine for the week was to ride the bus to school in the morning, attend classes until noon, tryout for the team until 5 o'clock in the evening, then catch the bus to return home.

On Friday, the last day of tryouts, without any fanfare, Coach Mac called me aside and offered me a two-year scholarship that covered my tuition, books, housing, and a work-study job. With the scholarship, the first part my dream had been fulfilled. I knew what my mission was, and I was determined to complete it.

For the next two years, I worked hard at being the best student athlete I could be at Odessa College. I never skipped class, and I kept my grades up. My work-study job was a real job. I worked for the tennis coach, and earned every dime I made. My teammates laughed at how hard I had to work.

My second year, I became a starter on the basketball team, and started every game during the season. By the end of the season, several second-year players received scholarships to a four-year institution. I did not. I was only averaging five points, five assists, six rebounds, and 2.5 steals per game. Coach Mac continually exhorted me to shoot more. It was my fault.

By April, I knew for sure that I wouldn't be getting a scholarship offer from a four-year institution. I resigned myself to following my old plan to complete my degree. I would find a job, work for a year, save my money, and then walk-on at a four-year institution.

That was my plan, until I received a letter from the Dean of Admissions requesting a meeting. His office opened at 8 a.m., but I got there at 7:15 a.m. I was sitting outside when he arrived.

"Are you Nathan?" the dean asked.

"Yes, sir."

He unlocked his door, and invited me in to have a seat.

"I think we have something for you," he said with a smile.

My heart started to pound as he picked up a folder that was resting on his desk.

He thumbed through some papers in the folder, then looked at me and asked: "Do you know you've earned enough credits to graduate from this school?"

"Yes, sir," I responded.

He looked further through the folder, then looked at me again and smiled.

He said: "We don't have many who have accomplished what you have: play ball for two full years, graduate, and carry a 3.0 GPA. Nathan, for your outstanding efforts, we're going to award you a full academic scholarship to any school in the state of Texas you wish to attend."

I decided to attend the University of North Texas (UNT).

In 1974, I graduated from UNT and went back to West Texas where I taught in the public school system for eighteen years. For ten years, I worked at Permian High School as a science teacher, assistant football coach, and administrator. After I was selected

Principal of the Year for Region 18, the *Odessa American* printed an article about me. One day I was shuffling through some paper in my office and Mrs. Mosley, my secretary, announced I had a visitor.

I didn't look up. I just told her to send him in. Suddenly, I felt a presence over me. When I looked up, Coach Wallace, my former coach, was standing there. He wasn't a coach anymore. He had become assistant superintendent of the school district where I had graduated.

I stood to shake his hand.

Instead, he gave me that same old big bear hug he used to give me years ago. I was overcome with emotion. I felt like that seventh-grade football player all over again. I couldn't stop crying.

Coach Wallace looked at me and said: "I just wanted to stop by and congratulate you on the achievement. We knew you would do this."

When I first met him at twelve years old, this man stood as a giant before me. I had grown into manhood myself, but he still seemed big—even bigger! It wasn't because of his height—it was because of his actions. It was because of his character.

I was now forty years old. Seeing Coach Wallace standing there, having taken the time to visit and affirm me yet again, made him even taller in my eyes.

Many years later, Coach Wallace still embodied and displayed the character I wanted to emulate and the legacy I want to walk out for the rest of my life.

# PART 3:
## My Legacy Stories

*Nate shows his skills playing basketball for Odessa College.*

# Chapter 7
# The Advantages of Disadvantages

*"For some reason, this is a very difficult lesson for us to learn. We have, I think, a very rigid and limited definition of what an advantage is. We think of things as helpful that actually aren't and think of other things as unhelpful that in reality leave us stronger and wiser."*

-*David and Goliath* by Malcolm Gladwell[1]

One of my greatest joys is seeing young people take the disadvantages that life has dealt them and turn them into life-enhancing advantages. I've had the opportunity throughout my coaching and teaching career to witness these changes in students on many occasions.

The main blessing is being able to play an active part in the transformation, and the students return to thank me for being there. I've worked with students of every ethnicity across every possible economic spectrum. When I see them complete the transformation, it always moves me to tears. I know that's why God put me on this earth.

When I graduated from college, I headed back to West Texas with grand plans for a coaching career. My thoughts were to get a job coaching at a high school in Odessa. I would coach football and teach science there for four or five years, and win a couple of State Championships in football or basketball.

After spending four or five years on the high school level, I would move on to coaching in the college ranks at a Division 1 school, again for about four to five years, and win a national championship in football or basketball. From there, it would be on to the NFL or NBA, where I would spend the remainder of my coaching career.

But God had other plans.

When I arrived back in Odessa in 1976, the oil boom was on and there were no teaching or coaching jobs. I enrolled in graduate school and worked two part-time jobs. I finally received a call from the head football coach at Ector High School asking if I was still looking for a job. I told him I was.

When he said he had an opening for an elementary school P.E. teacher, my first thought was: *Surely, you're joking! An elementary P.E. teacher!* After the initial shock wore off, I thought about how the two part-time jobs I held and graduate school were literally draining me. I took the job and decided to continue with graduate school.

In the '70s, Odessa had a serious after-school athletic program for elementary school students in grades four through six. The students competed against students across the city in various sporting activities including flag football, girls' volleyball, and both boys' and girls' teams for basketball, soccer, gymnastics, softball, and track and field. At the end of each sporting event, the athletic department would declare a City Champion and present a large trophy to the winning elementary school.

The school I was assigned to had many outstanding athletes. We competed for the City Championship in almost every sport. During my first year at the school, I met Maggie, a fourth-grader. Maggie was a great athlete and loved sports. She was from a large family with fourteen siblings. I believe she was either the eighth or ninth child in the family. The family was not well off. They lived in the lower socio-economic section of town, and her father worked manual labor jobs.

Maggie played all the girls sports after school. She was young, but I could tell she was a good athlete. She had a very competitive spirit. At the end of her fifth grade year, Maggie decided I was the best coach in the world and presented me with a plaque that stated as much. I found out from her teacher that she had saved all her money that summer to purchase the plaque for me. It moved me. (I still have it.)

During her sixth grade year, we won a couple of City Championships, due in large part to Maggie's efforts. She was a relentless competitor. When she finished sixth grade and entered junior high school, she often came over to visit me, and we talked about those days and the championship teams.

I could tell she was not doing well at home or in school. She constantly told me how much she hated school and she wasn't happy at home. There were afternoons when I would have to make her go home or I would take her there myself.

When she finished the eighth grade and moved on to high school, Maggie came by one afternoon to tell me she had met a young man, and they were in love. She said she was going to drop out of school and get married. I told her not to quit school and not to marry that young man. She did the exact opposite. She was so unhappy with school and her home life.

She still stayed in touch with me during the years she was married, but I could tell things weren't going well. One night she called me at 3:00 a.m. She said she was at a phone booth and asked if I could come get her and her children. When I arrived, she had on a tee shirt and shorts and her children were hurriedly dressed.

Her body was covered in bruises. She told me her husband had gotten drunk and they had a big fight. After the fight, he passed out. She said she knew she had to leave that night or she wouldn't make it out alive the next time. I took her and her children to her parents' house. A week later she called me and said she was filing for a divorce, and needed help.

I helped her. A few days later, she found a job and an apartment. She would call and I would visit with her at her job. She was struggling and depressed because of her situation, but she never gave up.

———— 66 ————————————

*When God puts someone in our path who needs our help, it is our responsibility to see it through. However, my help to Maggie began way back in grade four when I took the time to pay attention to her. A leader must see each student as an individual, not just as a mass of kids in his/her care.*

———————————————— 99 ————

During one of our visits, I told her not to get discouraged because she was a beautiful, smart, and determined young woman. I also told her that one day someone would come along who would admire all those qualities in her and ask her to be his wife. I asked her to do two things: Go back to school and get her GED; and start developing a relationship with Jesus.

She did both.

A year later, a young man came through and they struck up a friendship that turned into a serious relationship. He asked Maggie to marry him, and they moved to New Mexico. They started a very successful electrical business there and have lived happily together for twenty-five years.

Maggie has stayed in touch with me over the years. Two years ago, she called to say she was on her way to South Carolina for her brother's wedding. She was going to stop in the area, and she wanted her youngest daughter to meet me.

When they arrived, she called and gave me their hotel location. I drove over to meet them. When I walked into the lobby, Maggie and her daughter were sitting at a table. Maggie stood up and hugged me. Then she stepped back, with tears running down her cheeks, and said, "Coach Hearne, I want you to meet my youngest daughter. She's the only one that hasn't had a chance to meet you."

Her daughter, a beautiful young lady, looked a lot like her mother. She said, "We always thought our mother had you confused with Jesus. We said no human being on this earth could be all the things our mother said that you were."

Her daughter hugged me and said, "Thank you, for all you did for my mother."

Maggie posted this Facebook message on August 12, 2013—my birthday: *"I was thinking about my age when we first met and I was 10 years old, in the fourth grade. Wow! I'm going on 47 in October; that's 37 years. God has blessed me by putting you in my life for 37 years. Happy Birthday Coach!"*

*Coach Hearne poses for a photo on his way to football practice in the 1980s.*

# Chapter 8
# Transformational Coaching

---

*"One of the great myths in America is that sports build character. They can and they should. Indeed, sports may be the perfect venue in which to build character. But sports don't build character unless a coach possess character and intentionally teaches it."*
-*InSideOut Coaching* by Joe Ehrmann[1]

---

All across America, there are hundreds of public schools that have character-education programs in place. Unfortunately, a majority of these programs are generally ineffective.

The reason is no one has totally bought into the concept. In one room you have a teacher using every opportunity to teach character to students, but across the hall another teacher is using every class distraction as an opportunity to write a referral. They miss the opportunity to be transformational in the children's lives.

The number of economically disadvantaged and at-risk students entering the public schools across the state is increasing daily, and holistically we have nothing in place to address these issues. That has been, and will continue to be a problem.

If we truly want to see our children succeed, there are certain things that need to happen—beginning with the creation and implementation of statewide character-development programs in every school across the nation, on all grade levels, and in every content area—from pre-K through grade twelve. I hope that is something that will happen. But until then, each leader must continue to do what he or she can with the influence they've been given. As I've said, this doesn't apply to just teachers or coaches.

Parents, Sunday School teachers, grandparents, doctors, dentists, day care teachers, neighbors, all have somebody who is potentially looking up to them, and who they could positively influence.

Some teachers and coaches spend ungodly amounts of time lecturing economically disadvantaged children and meting out punishment when they misbehave, thinking it will bring about a change. But that's not the case. We need to nurture them in order to help them develop character. It's the most important thing we can do for them.

Scientific studies show that character strengths that matter the most when it comes to success for young people are not innate: they don't just pop up like a rabbit out of a magician's hat. These character traits are rooted in brain chemistry. The environment in which these young people live molds them.

If that's the case, it's clear what we have to do when it comes to character development in our children. Interventions that teach them what they need to know, in a supportive environment, using approaches like those I outline in this book, can develop these strengths and skills, starting at birth and going all the way through their college years. The question is, who will step up and assume the responsibility?

During my initial interview with Coach Gaines at Permian, he mentioned that he had called people in the community to question them about me.

The administrators, teachers, and people in the community knew me and they knew my work ethic. They also knew I loved and cared about the kids I coached. The kids' parents knew this as well. From my very first day teaching and coaching, I took responsibility for teaching character to my students.

I remember when I received a call from the head football coach at Ector High School—the minority high school. This was in

1980 and Odessa was still operating segregated public schools. Blackshear Jr. High school was predominantly Black and Hispanic. I was neither the principal's nor the head coaches' first choice. They'd had an open position that was initially given to another teacher who, it was later discovered, didn't have the completed credentials to accept the position. I was called as a desperate last resort.

I was asked if I was still interested in coaching football and I said an emphatic, "Yes!" I had been in the system for four years working as an elementary P.E. teacher and coach, but I knew I wanted to coach football on a higher level. My desire was to eventually coach high school football.

I didn't ask the question when they offered me the elementary job, but this time I had the foresight to ask how long I would have to stay at the junior high school.

"If you win in football with these kids, I'll move you up to the high school at the end of the year," he told me.

Without hesitation, I said I could do that.

## Only Thirteen Players

I didn't know how deeply I had stuck my foot in my mouth with my quick reply until I met with the vice principal, Mr. Joe Rutledge. He had already worked at the school for many years when I met him.

Mr. Rutledge was a great educator and visionary. Over the years, I grew to love him like a father. He served as an advocate, friend, and a mentor for me until the day he died. I'm indebted to him for the things he taught me, for the unconditional love he showed, and the legacy he left in the community for me and many others to follow. He was truly a great man!

During our meeting, Mr. Rutledge asked what the head coach

said about coaching the seventh grade football team. I repeated what he had said to me.

"He's setting you up for failure," Mr. Rutledge told me. "It's hard to get these kids to come out for football; the numbers are too small. They'll come out for basketball, but it's hard to get them out for football."

Then, he asked if I had a master's degree. I said, "Yes, sir."

He repeated himself: "He's setting you up for failure. He's not going to bring you up to the high school next year. Especially if you have more education than him."

Mr. Rutledge told me to report to the field house to visit with the head ninth grade coach. When I arrived and saw the condition of the equipment and the locker room, my heart sank. It was a mess. The jerseys, shoulder pads, helmets, and shoes were in terrible condition. So was the locker room. They had old universal gym equipment, with all the cables broken. Weights were scattered all around the locker room.

The Ector County ISD wasn't interested in providing updated facilities or new equipment to south side schools during those days. I went to the local athletic supply store and asked the manager for a line of credit. He agreed. I bought some cables to fix the universal gym, and I picked up some basic apparel—socks, T-shirts, and jock straps for the future players.

The first day of school, the players milled around outside the field house talking and laughing. I was assigned the Gold Team and another coach was assigned the Green Team. Thirty-two kids showed up to play football.

I began to understand what Mr. Rutledge was talking about. Winning with only sixteen players could be a challenge. We divided the players; I picked sixteen for the Gold Team and he picked sixteen for his Green Team. We had two weeks to get them ready for their first ball game.

Despite the setbacks in numbers, the poor facilities, and inadequate equipment, I was excited about getting my first opportunity to coach football. This is what I had always wanted to do. I was a bit overzealous the first week. On Friday, three players turned their uniforms in. That left me with thirteen boys. To be factual, it was only eleven because my two subs had never played any organized sport. The other coaches on the staff razzed me. They said if I kept coaching like that I would have to forfeit all my games before the season started. We were required to suit up at least eleven players; I was scraping the bottom of the barrel.

## The Season

I knew I had to have them ready to play soon, but it was turning out to be a slow process. I didn't have enough bodies to work with, and I needed more time. I asked the head ninth grade coach if I could work my kids out on Saturday. I remember him smiling and saying, "Coach they're your players, do what you want to do. But I can tell you this—they're not going to come to practice on Saturday. They'll be at the Boys Club playing basketball."

I told my kids on Friday that we would have practice on Saturday, and I would come to their homes and pick them up. I had an old faded red and white 1965 Step Side Ford pickup. I started out that Saturday morning at 6 a.m. But before I picked up any of the players, I went to the Southern Maid Donut Shop and bought six dozen fresh donuts. After that, I went to the local supermarket and bought five gallons of orange juice. When they saw those donuts and orange juice, they got excited. We had a great practice. I held practice on Saturday for the rest of that season and not a single player missed.

In the first game of the season, I remember standing across

the field looking at the opposing team—Hood Junior High. Their coach was Mike Belew. Mike and I would later coach together at Permian High School. But we didn't know each other on that day. Over the years, we've reminisced about that game and each time he tells the story, his team gets smaller and smaller. But I remember him having twice as many players as I did.

As I stood there looking across the field, one of my players eased up beside me and tugged on my shirt. I looked down, it was Curly Alford, my cornerback and the smallest player on the team. Pointing his finger at the other team and making a long sweeping motion from one end to the other, he asked: "Coach, are we going to have to play all of them?"

I looked down at him and said, "Yes sir, and you know what? We're going to beat them!"

We beat Mike's team that day, and it wasn't even a close game.

Following that game we continued winning until we stood at the top of the division with a 5-0 record, and had an opportunity to win the division championship against Crockett Junior High. They were also 5-0.

Crockett had a large number of players. They were well-coached. I remember arriving to play the game and getting off the bus with those thirteen warriors. The head ninth grade coach was there to greet me with one of his players at his side. We shook hands. He pointed out our halftime facility. I remember thanking him and walking off, but I overheard the player standing beside him say, "Coach, if that's all he has, our team is going to kill them."

The game started and they marched down the field and scored on us with the first possession. This had never happened to us before. We held all our previous opponents to only six points per game, and no one had ever scored on us with the first possession.

I knew this was going to be a tough ball game, and that we might not get out with a "W." I called my players to the sideline.

"It feels like you've just been gut-punched. Do we get off the canvas and answer the bell, or do we lie down and wallow in the pain?" I challenged them.

I could tell by the look in their eyes they were going to fight and we weren't going to lie down for anyone.

We eventually scored and tied the ball game 6-6. The skies had been overcast and dark the whole day. We kicked the ball and made the stop on the return. They lined up to run the next offensive play and we lined up to play defense. In that moment, those gray dark skies broke open.

The thunder rumbled and the rain came down in sheets. I couldn't see my players, but I heard a whistle and a referee came running toward me waving a yellow flag. He was shouting, "Game over! Game over, Coach! Tie ball game. Tie ball game!"

I stood there in the rain and lifted my face to the heavens. I stretched my arms out wide and said, "Thank you, God!"

## The City Championship

The next week, Crockett lost their last ballgame. We won ours and stood at the top of the division as champions with a record of 6-0-1. The following week we prepared for the City Championship game against Nimitz Junior High. They were the affluent north side school. They had good coaches, nice equipment, great facilities, and lots of good athletes who participated in their football program.

We played them on their field. When we arrived, they had a sizable number of players suited up for the game. They had on sparkling white and blue uniforms and we stepped off the bus wearing tattered hand-me-downs. Rich versus poor. It was classic.

I had pushed the kids hard during practice that week and told them repeatedly to prepare for a serious dogfight. Truthfully, I didn't doubt my players' ability to win; they were that good. My concern was Nimitz's numbers. Their ability to keep fresh players on the field might eventually wear us down.

I preached to them the whole week not to give up, not to quit when things turn bad, to stay focused, and play defense. I wanted the Nimitz coach and his players to know that we would not lay down, that we were there for the duration, and we were going to fight until the final seconds ran off the clock.

My players gave me that and much, much more. They played with amazing heart and character that day. Their play would be indicative of how they would respond during their playing careers at Permian. They were relentless the whole game—they never gave up, and never stopped fighting. At every setback, they'd regroup and come back again and again.

The final score was Nimitz 20 and Blackshear 6, but the score will never be a true indicator of what took place during that game. There were four flags thrown during the game—all against us—and they called back two of our touchdowns. The official wouldn't let us get any momentum.

After the game we got on the bus. The kids couldn't hold it, and broke down crying. It hurt them so badly to lose. It was painful for me, as well. I never said anything to them about the officiating. I only spoke of how proud I was of the way they played.

It touched my heart to see eleven kids play against those odds and never quit, and never complain. They just kept grinding it out. To see them cry because they didn't win spoke volumes to me about their character. It doesn't matter what level; junior high, high school, college or the professional level. It was an indicator of character, leadership, and talent.

I could have let them see how I was frustrated with the officiating. But I didn't want to give them an excuse.

— 66 —————————————

*Sometimes you do the right things, play your heart out, and will not win the trophy. There are things beyond your control. As I learned throughout my career, sometimes the agendas of others get in the way. But as a leader, I didn't want my kids to see me making up excuses. I wanted them to continue to be built up in who they were, and affirmed for their hard work.* 99 —

During their high school careers, five players from the team would continue to play football and contributed to Permian's 1984 and 1985 State Championships playoff appearance. Permian won one and lost one. Two of the five were named First Team All-State at their positions.

After the season, Mr. Rutledge called me to his office and asked me how I was able to win with thirteen players when many others before me complained. I said, "Mr. Rutledge, you know the environment these kids have grown up in. All they see is violence, death, and drugs. But if you nurture them and affirm them for who they are, they'll do some amazing things. I let them know that I cared for them and loved them. I worked them hard and made them believe their hard work equals success. And I gave them something to believe in—a goal that was much bigger than themselves. I told them they could win a championship with just thirteen players."

I also said, "Mr. Rutledge, when you have kids who know hard times and have great athleticism, and you give them something to believe in—they'll accomplish what some people deem impossible."

My desire during the season was to help those young men believe in their abilities. I wanted to see their lives transformed. I wanted them to dedicate themselves to a single purpose and achieve it. If it happened, it would carry over into other areas of their lives. It happened for me, and it could happen for them.

# Chapter 9
# It's Bigger than MOJO

*"As a school, most whites never had much use for Ector ... It was on the Southside, and the less heard about the area, the better. 'I think the [white] community perceived it as a minority place, a place they wouldn't travel into,' said Jim Moore. [Ector's last principal.] ... But with Ector's closing, [whites] suddenly began to see enormous value in some of its black students. It had nothing to do with their academic potential."*

*-Friday Night Lights* by H.G. Bissinger[1]

All my life I've been around black athletes who either didn't think making good grades was important, or take their education seriously. During my collegiate career, I witnessed many of my teammates spending more study time playing spades, dominos, and shooting pool than in the library.

That was in the '70s, but it's not much better today. As a matter of fact, it may be worse. Over 78 percent of black teenage males are living in single parent homes. The graduation rate for black males in America is only 52 percent, and black males between the ages of 19 and 29 make up 75 percent of the prison population in this country.

At Permian, I was on a mission to change those statistics and that perception. And I was not alone. Mrs. Patricia Rogers, a business teacher and Pepette sponsor at the school, was as adamant as I was about these young men getting good grades. She was a tremendous help in letting me know which players were losing their focus in the classroom. She grew up on the south side and knew the community well. Any time players got into trouble off-campus, she would let me know and I would address it with them.

She was a tremendous help!

Mr. Rutledge, the vice principal, Mrs. Estella Willard, a black English teacher at the school, and many others in the black community also cared. Yes, there were those in the community who thought their time was better spent trying to bring me down on recruiting violations, but there were many, many others in the community who knew my heart and helped me.

## Venshard Dobbins

After I left coaching football at Permian for the job in administration, I continued trying to help the players on the team as much as I could in my new role. A long-time friend and colleague, Mrs. Dalila Weeks, also an assistant principal at the school, called me one day and asked if I knew the whereabouts of Venshard Dobbins. Dalila had coached for many years in the district. I had known her for twenty-five years. We first met as elementary P.E. teachers in the '70s and both moved to the junior high coaching ranks. We both were now working together as administrators at Permian.

She had the same heart for helping the students as I did.

She called me and said she hadn't seen Venshard in school in almost three weeks. I was shocked. She said she couldn't find him, and that everyone she asked had no clue as to his whereabouts.

Dalila knew Venshard and I had a close relationship, and she believed that if anyone could find him, I could. She advised me that if he wasn't back in school immediately, he could lose everything. A full scholarship was hanging in the balance.

Skipping school was totally out of character for Venshard. I had coached him in football and basketball. He was bright, gifted, and athletic. He was a National Honor Society student in line to receive a scholarship. It was April of his senior year, and he would be graduating soon. This was a dire situation.

I knew Odessa and I had a number of people I could call on who would help me find Venshard. I had a good idea where to start, so I searched the community looking for him. I wondered what would cause him to do such a thing?

Finally, information came back to me that I could find him in an apartment complex on the south side. After questioning some of the tenants, I was able to locate the exact apartment.

Venshard answered the door when I knocked. Our eyes locked, and I could see the look of relief and yet pain at the same time. He was relieved that I was standing in his doorway—he knew how much I loved him and my presence represented a sense of security. But he was in pain—from whatever had caused him to miss school for three weeks.

"Coach!" he said.

I hugged him, and he invited me in.

"Venshard," I said, "what's going on? You haven't been to school in three weeks!"

"I've got some problems, Coach," he said. "My mother just left me here and moved away." He looked at me with sad eyes.

"Why would she do that, Coach?" he wondered aloud.

I didn't want to speculate into any issues regarding his mother's behavior. I knew there would be an opportunity for him and his mother to work through those dynamics one day. I said truthfully, "Venshard, I don't know. But I do know this: You can't continue to miss school. You have too much to lose!"

He dropped his head. I waited. I wanted to give him as much time as he needed to think about his life and the decision he was going to make at that moment. I didn't probe him into why his mother would choose to leave him in an apartment by himself, at such a crucial time in his life. I suspected he really didn't know.

Venshard was an amazing young man; good-looking with a big bright smile. He was loyal, analytical, and compassionate. If you were his friend, he'd stand in the gap for you—no matter what the circumstance. It was hard for me to imagine what caused this, but my goal was to get him back in school as quickly as possible.

"You can live with me and my wife for as long as you like," I told him. "I'll take care of you."

When I said that, he gave me a look that expressed he was deeply moved and completely overwhelmed by the offer. His eyes expressed, "You would do something like that for me?"

After further thoughtful dialogue, Venshard said, "Coach, I have an older sister I can contact. I'll call her tomorrow. I think she might be able to help me."

"I won't press you," I said, "but I want you in school tomorrow. You can't miss another day!"

He responded by saying, "Yes sir, Coach, I'll be there."

Venshard was back in school the next day and didn't miss again. He graduated with honors from Permian, received an academic/athletic scholarship to attend a school in Missouri. Today, he is married, has a beautiful family, and is an elder in his church. Venshard and his mother have reconciled, and have a very close relationship.

Venshard has maintained contact with me over the years. He calls me periodically just to say hi. He credits me with being that father figure who was always there when he needed help.

Venshard Dobbins used that disadvantage he experienced and turned it into a series of abundant blessings. From the very first day I met him, I knew he had great potential.

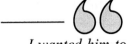

*I wanted him to know I loved him like a son, and that I was willing to intervene for him any time he needed me. When he was lost, I went after him. A good leader will go after the lost. It's what Jesus did for us.*

## John Williams

John was our tailback on the 1991 State Championship team. He rushed for 1,200 yards, and our fullback, Malcolm Hamilton, rushed for 1,800 yards. They were a tough combination for any opposing team to stop.

John started on varsity as a sophomore, which is an indicator that he was one heck of a running back. During his junior year, he came out of the shoot running, even harder than he did as a sophomore. He was a seasoned veteran now and known across the state. He was receiving offer letters from numerous universities.

I was John's grade-level principal, and part of my job was to make sure students stayed on track to graduate. The NCAA had changed its rule for eligibility. There were two changes made which would gravely affect John's ability to stay on track to receive an athletic scholarship.

I reviewed John's transcript and he was taking Basic English. He would have to be moved to regular English to be eligible. Also, the required score for athletes on the ACT and SAT College entrance exams had been increased. We had to address these requirements if John was to receive a scholarship.

John was raised by a single mother, and had one older sister. It was important to his mom that John and his sister receive a quality education. She knew her son was a great athlete and had the potential for an athletic scholarship. She wanted to make sure he was on track to do that.

I called John and his mother in for a meeting to give them the news. I laid out the plan and told them what we would have to do the next two years to keep him on track to receive a scholarship. As always, Miss Williams was very supportive.

This plan would require John to work hard at improving his reading and writing skills. John was intelligent and a very hard worker. I had no doubt he could do this.

I promised John and his mother that I would stand by him, and get him all the support he needed. John promised he wouldn't quit on me, and that he would keep me informed of his progress. He did that. We talked often.

The news didn't sit well with the coaching staff that John's classes were being switched up. Coach Belew, John's position coach, came to see me. He was upset that I had taken John out of the Basic English class and moved him to regular English. They thought it was going to be a distraction for John and have adverse effects on his playing.

Mike said the one positive thing John had in this world was playing football. I could tell he was genuinely concerned for John's well-being, and I appreciated that.

"If we take that (football) away from him, he has nothing," Mike said. "If you move John out of Basic English, it will destroy him."

I didn't go into a lot of detail with Mike that day. I just said, "Mike, if I don't move John out of that class and put him in regular English, his life really will be destroyed. He can do it."

I could tell he wasn't pleased with my answer, but he didn't say anything and left the office. No other coaches came to see me about it.

My intent was never to hurt the team or the coaching staff—the kids on the team were special to me and the coaching staff were like family. We had been through a lot together—but I had to make the call. It was the right thing to do.

I thought about the ramifications if I didn't do all I could to help John receive a scholarship once his playing career was over at Permian. I knew Mike didn't have a complete picture to understand it all. John had the ability in him. It was going to take some extra work, but he could do it. I was that confident he could make it happen.

Experience showed that people went out of their way to look for negative news to spread about the Permian football team. To have one of their top players ineligible would be great headlines for the opposition. I concentrated my efforts on making sure that didn't happen in John's case.

John finished his career as one of the top rushers in school history—almost 5,000 total yards in a three-year career. He passed his English classes, his ACT Exam, and received a full scholarship to play at Texas Christian University.

Years later, Mike and I discussed this event and he said, "I'm sorry, I didn't know what you were doing."

"I know," I told him.

Leaders must take the full picture into account when making decisions for those in their care.

## Sheldon Bass

I had the opportunity to work with Sheldon as both a coach and as an administrator. During my time as the junior varsity basketball coach, Sheldon came out for the team. His father was an outstanding athlete who had played at Ector High School. He loved sports. Sheldon was like his father; he, too, loved sports, and he loved competing.

Sheldon came out for basketball after the football season was over. I usually gave the football players a little time to get acclimated before I put them on the court for any length of time during a game. Two days after Sheldon came out for the basketball team, he wrote me a three-page letter begging me to let him start in a game. He was that competitive! Once he got on the court, his motor never stopped running.

Sheldon was a varsity athlete as a sophomore. He played cornerback for Permian on the '91 State Championship team. He could flat-out play the game. He had this uncanny ability to anticipate when and where the ball would be thrown. He had great vision, great hands, and a great instinct for the ball.

Sheldon had the privilege of being reared by both his parents—Mr. and Mrs. William Hill. They were very supportive. They knew he was gifted and would receive a Division 1 offer after he graduated. The offer letters were coming in daily.

But there was a problem. They had been notified by Sheldon's counselor at the school that he would be half a credit short on his transcript. Investigation into the matter showed that the half credit was a typographical error committed at the junior high school he attended.

I was Sheldon's grade level principal at the time. This information was presented to the principal, who said he couldn't do anything about it. I could understand his reservation. The school had been placed on probation twice for UIL infractions. It was making everyone a little skittish.

Mr. and Mrs. Hill were not happy with that decision and requested a meeting with me. I knew the Hills well. They were good people who worked hard and wanted the best for their son. They explained the situation and I promised to take care of

Sheldon.

I called Mr. Robert McCarley, the principal of the junior high school Sheldon had attended. He had a thirty-year service record in the district. He was an outstanding administrator and a gracious man. He said he would be happy to assist me with the problem. He said he loved Sheldon and would do anything to help him.

We came up with a plan. We called the NCAA Clearinghouse. They gave specific guidelines as to how we could correct the typographical error on the transcript. We followed the guidelines to the letter and submitted it back to them. A couple of weeks later, they confirmed that the corrections had been accepted and approved by the NCAA.

Sheldon and his parents were ecstatic over the news. He went on to complete an outstanding career at Permian. He graduated and received an athletic scholarship to attend Texas Tech University. When Sheldon was a freshman, he started as a receiver for Tech. He was that good!

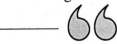

*A good leader needs to be persistent. Things don't get done by themselves. Kids take note when someone is persistent on their behalf. It is a quality that, when modeled, can have lasting impact on the character development of our youth.*

## Nick Keeton

Nick was the starting quarterback on the '92 Permian team. I really liked him. He was an excellent leader. He was the prototypical Permian quarterback—smart , confident, hardworking, and humble.

Mrs. Keeton called me one day and asked if she could meet

with me. She said it was concerning Nick's chemistry class. We met and she expressed her concern over Nick's ability to pass the class. I listened, thanked her for coming, and told her I would check into it. As an administrator, I wanted to gather all the facts before making a decision about the best solution to Mrs. Keeton's concern.*

I made an appointment with the teacher. I was given the course content, the grading guidelines, and the expectations of the students. I thanked him for his time. I called Nick to my office, and mentioned I had spoken with both his mother and his chemistry teacher.

I now needed to hear from Nick. I wanted to see his average in the class, evidence of the assignments he had completed, and what his concerns were regarding the class. Nick never said a negative word about the teacher, nor did he make excuses regarding his ability or inability to pass the class. Nick was a hardworking young man. On the practice field and during the games, I never heard him make excuses or place blame on his teammates for bad snaps, dropped passes, or fumbled hand-offs. He was exactly what you wanted in a quarterback.

After weighing all the facts, I went to his counselor and told her to make a schedule change. I thought Nick would be better off in a different class. The teacher didn't like it. He went to the head coach and threatened to report me to the UIL for transferring Nick out of the class to keep him eligible.

The head coach told me what the teacher said. I simply explained to him that keeping Nick eligible was not the basis of my decision. I made my decision based on what I felt was the best

---

* Three of the four Permian football players that I've mentioned in this chapter are black. Nick Keeton is white. I included Nick's story to show that my desire was to help every student that needed me. I was never motived to help students based upon the color of their skin.

learning environment for Nick. I felt, if the teacher wanted to turn me in to the UIL for that, it was his prerogative.

The teacher's threat was supposed to scare me because of what I had been through before. I wasn't intimidated. Nick had the same rights as any other student. Being the quarterback on the Permian football team didn't diminish his rights.

I had used that same procedure with many other students and parents requesting schedule changes. I investigated the request and, based on my findings, I made any needed changes. We'd be foolish to think all teachers are the same. Some students learn better under different teachers. The situation was never mentioned to me again. Nick had a great season and flourished with his new chemistry teacher. Nick's mother was thankful that someone took the time to care. (On page 141 you can read a letter she wrote to the principal about this situation.)

The academic problems the players experienced were very important to me. If I didn't address the academic issues, everything else was a moot point. I wasn't trying to please everyone with my decisions; I wanted the students to be successful. If there was anything I could do to help them, I was going to do it. I wanted the players and their parents to know academic success was much bigger than MOJO.

Parents are the best resource for making interventions in their children's lives, but they are not the only resource. Transforming interventions can come from social workers, teachers, coaches, clergy members, pediatricians, and even a next-door neighbor.

*Dr. Hearne speaks to kids of all ages. Pictured above, Dr. Hearne brings a challenge to a high school graduating class. Below, he shares valuable life lessons with elementary-aged students.*

# Chapter 10
# Make Lemonade

---

*"If you have a lemon, make a lemonade."*
*-How to Stop Worrying and Start Living*
by Dale Carnegie[1]

---

Mistakes and failures are a part of life. Romans 3:23 states, *"For all have sinned and fall short of the glory of God." (HCSB)*

I also believe that failure becomes permanent if we decide to make it permanent. Romans 6:23 says, *"For the wages of sin is death, but the gift of God is eternal life in Christ Jesus our Lord."* (HCSB)

For many years, I've taught that concept to the students I've had the privilege to coach and teach. I believe when we properly apply ourselves, when we do what we know is right and we do it with faith, when we put Jesus first and trust Him to direct our steps, then failures are just another obstacle we have to overcome. They aren't permanent. They are stepping stones and building blocks to success.

During my second year in administration, my belief in this concept was seriously tested. I arrived home late one Saturday evening to discover several phone messages from the school's cheerleader sponsor. She said no matter how late it was when I got the message, I was to call her.

I called and she said they had made a mistake in the cheerleader tryouts. She said she had failed to check the grades of all the students and some had been selected who were not eligible.

I was the junior class grade-level principal and the cheerleaders were part of my responsibility.

She wanted to know if we, including the principal, could meet as soon as possible to discuss the "mistake." Whenever I hear the word mistake, I think: *Admit it, correct it, and don't repeat it.* We all make mistakes. My suggestion was to do the tryouts over. That suggestion was rejected.

The principal decided to pass the decision to the superintendent, who decided to pass it on to the School Board. The School Board asked one question—How many tried out for cheerleader?

Thirty-five to forty girls had tried out. They decided to make them all cheerleaders. When this news was released, pandemonium broke out. That decision put us in the national headlines as well. Newspapers across the nation carried the story.

This was MOJO. When you mentioned that name, the media felt it was always worth reporting. The phones at the school were ringing off the hook. I started receiving numerous calls from parents. Mrs. Mosley entered my office and said, "Mr. Hearne, you have twenty phone messages."

Recognizing the gravity of the situation, the principal told me to have all the calls regarding the cheerleaders directed to his office. That was on a Monday. During that week, two cheerleaders' mothers got into a verbal confrontation in the office and had to be physically separated. The cheerleaders were being referred to around the school as the "Real Cheerleaders" and "Not Real Cheerleaders."

During one practice, a cheerleader was accidentally dropped and broke her collarbone. The fighting amongst the cheerleaders had become so divisive that one student, who was not a "Real Cheerleader," asked me to have her name removed from the list.

She said it was all too stressful.

On Friday, the principal informed me that he was turning the situation back over to me. I had a meeting at the central administration building that afternoon. When the meeting was over, I stopped by my wife's office. She was the Director over Guidance and Counseling for the district at the time.

I told her what happened, and that the cheerleader situation was now back in my hands. She asked me what I was going to do. I didn't know.

We were engaging in small talk when I noticed a plaque on her desk that read: *"When life gives you lemons, make lemonade."* — *Author unknown.*

An idea hit me like a rush.

"That's it!" I said to my wife. "We're going to have church. These are all God-fearing, upstanding parents who love, support, and really want to do the right thing for their children. We're going to have church."

"They won't come to our church," my wife insisted.

"I'm not asking them to come to our church. We'll do it at the school in the auditorium."

"You can't do that. They'll fire you!"

"What a way to go," I answered.

I hurried out of her office and headed back to the school. I had Mrs. Mosley call all the cheerleaders and their parents and tell them to be at a meeting in the auditorium at 7:00 p.m. I was amazed they all showed up, with the exception of one set of parents who said they didn't want to participate.

I took my Bible with me, and at the beginning of the meeting I read a scripture to them. I read: *"Jesus said, 'Greater love has no one than this, that someone lay down his life for his friends.'"* *(John 15:12 ESV)*

Then, I said to them, "Your children attend one of the most recognized schools in the nation. No other high school generates the kind of attention that MOJO does, be it positive or negative.

"We have just been given a basketful of lemons by the School Board. The media, all across this nation, are mocking us and using this incident to make us look bad in the eyes of people from the east coast to the west coast. Let me read again: Jesus said, 'No greater love has someone than to lay down one's life for one's friend.'"

These were all very prominent citizens—leaders—well-established members of the community.   They were there to support their children.

I went on:

*"Your children are an extension of you. If you're mad and upset about this at home, your children will be mad and upset about this situation at school.   But if you're calm, patient, and show a willingness to work through this mistake, then they will do the same thing at school. You're their greatest influence."*

Their children were sitting on the front row as I stood before them.

"I do not see any of your children being career cheerleaders," I said. "What I see before me are future doctors, lawyers, teachers, bankers, and business owners. They will not be career cheerleaders. I'm asking you today to die to self and lay down your lives for your children. Let's take this situation, this sour basketful of lemons that we've been given, and turn it into pitchers full of sweet, refreshing lemonade."

The parents responded positively to my message. They shook my hand and thanked me for having the meeting. The next day I received calls, cards, letters, and even flowers. The family that said they didn't want to attend called and apologized for missing the meeting.

I knew the parents didn't want to see their children suffering because of this situation. They wanted to bring an end to it, and they did. They needed guidance to put the situation in perspective. That is what a good leader does.

## Your Worst Nightmare

In the mid to late '80s and early '90s I taught biology at Permian High School. I had a student in my fourth period class who left an impression on me. She was a quiet, reserved, intelligent young lady with an aura of calmness that made you feel a sense of peace when you were around her.

She entered my class early on the first day neatly dressed. I soon discovered if homework assignments were due—her assignments would be first in the basket. She was an A-B student. She had beautiful handwriting and her work was meticulous.

The first six weeks was perfect, she continued her early arrivals and handed in homework assignments early. Some days she would finish her homework during class and hand it in before the end of the period. The first six weeks, she was a straight-A student.

During the second six weeks, I noticed a change. It started subtly. I noticed on her homework assignments she would leave some questions blank. That didn't happen on any of the work she turned in during the first six weeks. She also started turning in some of her assignments late. As the weeks progressed, there were times she didn't turn in her assignments at all, and she missed class. I was coaching football and didn't have time to really visit with her like I wanted to.

When the second six-week period came to an end, all her grades were failing and she had missed a number of days from school. I decided to ask her other teachers if they noticed a change in her behavior, and they all said the same thing. They agreed that there was a drastic change from the first to the second six weeks, and she was failing their classes as well.

One day I was coming back from lunch, on my way to practice, and I discovered the reason for the drastic change. There was a convenience store across the street from the school, where many of the students hung out for lunch. I saw her with a former student I knew was not going to be a positive influence in her life.

He had dropped out of school, was into the drug scene, and, in my opinion, had only one mission in mind for her. He was older by two or three years. She was naïve and likely had never experienced anyone as smooth and manipulative as him.

Early one morning, I was on my way from the office after picking up my class rosters when I saw her sitting in the cafeteria by herself. I walked over and asked her to come with me back to the room, because I needed to have a conference with her about her grades and attendance.

Once in the room, I asked her to have a seat. I didn't waste any time getting to the point.

I said to her, "Do you know you're failing my class, and that you will not be able to graduate if you fail this class?"

She nodded.

This moment was very important and I didn't want to miss any opportunity I had to help her. I had a feeling something was wrong.

"You've missed a lot of my classes," I continued. "I've

checked with your other teachers and they all say the same thing—that there's been a drastic change in your behavior and you are failing their classes as well. And I think I know the reason. I saw you with the young man last week. I know him.

"You need to know this: He's not the kind of guy you take home to your parents. He isn't looking to ask you to go to the prom with him. He only wants one thing from you, and as soon as he accomplishes his mission, he's moving on to the next conquest."

I finished by saying, "I would not classify this young man as the man of your dreams. I believe this young man will turn out to be your worst nightmare."

When I was done, she dropped her head, folded her arms across her stomach, and laid her head on the desk. I saw her tears fall from her face onto the desk. I knew then I had struck a very sensitive nerve, and there was something very painful happening in her life.

I told her, "I don't know what's happening in your life, but I do know this: There is nothing that's happening that's too big for God. There is nothing too bad for God to forgive. God loves you unconditionally, and there is nothing you can do to stop that love. Whatever is going on with you, I want you to know also that I'm here to help you with it."

I picked up a box of tissue and put it on the desk in front of her. She lifted her head, sat up straight in her desk, took a couple of tissues, and wiped her eyes. Then she stood up, thanked me and walked out of the room.

I never saw her at school again.

A week later, I received a withdrawal notice from the office with her name on it. She had withdrawn from school.

*I blew that one!* I thought to myself.

Almost three years later, when I was working as an

administrator, Mrs. Mosley knocked on my door and said I had some visitors. I asked her to show them in.

As I looked up, in walked a young woman with a small child that was about two or three years old. I stood and offered her a seat.

"Do you remember me?" she asked.

I didn't.

"I wanted to come by and thank you for helping me," she said.

"I helped you?" I asked.

"You saw me in the cafeteria that day and asked to speak with me," she began. "My mother had kicked me out of the house. That guy you saw me with, when I told him I was pregnant, he said he didn't want to see me again.

"When you told me that there's nothing too big for God to forgive, that God loved me unconditionally, and that you were willing to help me, I knew what I needed to do. I needed to go back home and talk this over with my mother. We decided I would keep my baby. I transferred to the alternative school, finished my classes early, and earned my diploma. I had my baby, and shortly afterward I enrolled in the nursing program at the Junior College. I have one semester left before I graduate.

"I just wanted to stop by and let you know I really appreciate you being there for me," she said. "You were the only one of my teachers who mentioned anything about God."

This young lady had been given a basket filled with sour lemons, and she decided to do the bold, courageous thing: she decided to make lemonade.

# Chapter 11
# The Best Job in Town

---

*"Early adversity, scientists have come to understand, not only affects the conditions of children's lives, it can also alter the physical development of their brains. But innovative thinkers around the country are now using the knowledge to help children overcome the constraints of poverty. With the right support, children who grow up in the most painful circumstances can go on to achieve amazing things."*
*-How Children Succeed* by Paul Tough[1]

---

I resigned from Permian in 1995 and enrolled in seminary at Southern Methodist University (SMU). In April of my first year there, the District Superintendent of the Methodist Church from the East Texas Conference called me. He said he was on campus looking for a student-pastor to serve a small, black Methodist church in Clarksville. He had gotten my phone number from another seminarian at SMU. I would estimate the population to be around 3,000 in Clarksville at the time. Working at Walmart would be considered gainful employment in the community.

The student population was mostly white, but not by much. I'd say the black student population was around forty-five percent, with a small percentage of Hispanic students.

He wanted to know if he and his wife could take me to lunch to discuss the possibilities of my serving the church. I accepted the invitation. While waiting to be served our meals, he told me he wanted to be honest with me and put all his cards on the table.

He said the church was struggling with its membership. The

church couldn't afford to pay a pastor, but the conference would help supplement the pastor's salary.

The superintendent said he couldn't find anyone on campus who wanted to pastor the church. My name was mentioned on several occasions as a possible candidate whenever he asked for a referral. He paused, looked at me and said, "You're my last hope. If you don't take it, they will not have a pastor."

I told him I would have to talk it over with Callie.

He gave me pictures of the church and the congregation, and asked me to share them with Callie. I called her and we discussed the advantages and disadvantages of the offer. We decided I would accept the position.

Shortly afterward, Callie called and said the superintendent from the Odessa public school system wanted to speak with me. I flew home to meet with him and he offered me the position of summer school principal at Permian.

I accepted it. The word 'busy' took on a whole new meaning.

During that summer, I served as principal at Permian through the week and pastor of St. Paul United Methodist Church in Clarksville on the weekend. Callie, our son, and I left Odessa on every Friday and drove for twelve hours to get to the church. I prepared my sermons on Saturday, addressed any needs the members had, and preached on Sunday.

We arrived back in Odessa around 1 a.m. on Monday, and I was up by 5 a.m. to prepare for school. That was my routine for the summer.

As I was being introduced by the conference superintendent as their new pastor, I noticed two white gentlemen slip into the back of the church and sit quietly. They stood out because this was an all-black congregation. The only other whites present were the superintendent and his wife. Once the introductions were over, the two men came forward.

One identified himself as Superintendent of the Clarksville Independent School District, and the other was head coach of the football team. They said they had heard I was coming to town and it was public knowledge that I had coached football at Permian High School. The superintendent asked if I would be willing to help coach their football team. The head coach said they would love to have me.

"We haven't won but one game each year for the past nine years," the superintendent said.

This was intriguing to me, but I was there to pastor the church, and I was still taking classes at SMU. I looked at the church superintendent, who told me whatever I decided was fine with him.

The chairman of the Church Council spoke up, saying: "It's alright with us; besides we need a football coach much worse than we need a pastor."

I looked at my wife, who said, "If they need you to coach the team, it's OK with me."

"I'm still taking classes at SMU, and I don't know if I'll have time to teach a class, coach the team, pastor the church, and continue with my studies," I told the superintendent and head coach.

"You don't have to teach a class," the superintendent said. "We'll pay you a stipend just to coach."

A week later, I was introduced to the staff and the football team. The head coach had hired three new coaches. One was Virgil Crow, who eventually became a close friend. In fact, after our time coaching together at Clarksville, Virgil became a head coach elsewhere and often invited me to speak to his team during pre-game and halftime.

When I met the Clarksville players, I could tell that as a whole, they were a talented group of young men. I saw no reason why they shouldn't win. Clarksville was a very small school district. There were only 300 students in the school's ninth through twelfth grades. Thirty-two players made up the varsity football team.

There was work to be done before the season started.

In my years of coaching, I always had a dual role. I served as the offensive and defensive line coach, and the strength and conditioning coach. I always had an eye for weight rooms—how they should be set up and operated. The weight room at Clarksville High School needed some serious attention. We had rearranging and cleaning to do. From my experiences, the weight room had always been the place where you changed boys into men, dreams into reality, and losers into champions.

We worked them hard during two-a-day practices and the pre-season.

The season began, and we lost the first game by two points. It was a hard-fought battle. I thought the kids played well. The next game we won, but the two games after that we lost. In one game, we were blown out by fifty points.

After the game on Friday night, the coaching staff met on Saturday mornings at the field house to break down game film and to game-plan for the next week. On the way to the field house I usually stopped at the local convenience store and picked up coffee and donuts.

The store had a small breakfast area where you could sit, eat, and chat if you wanted to. There was usually a group of men from the community sitting around the table drinking coffee and talking. I knew they knew me, and I knew I was probably a topic of their conversations on those Saturday mornings.

I entered the store, ordered my coffee and donuts, and turned to leave. One of the men stood up and approached me as I was leaving.

"Are you that MOJO coach?" he asked.

Obviously, he already knew who I was when he asked the question. In a town that small, there was probably very little he didn't know about me.

"I coached football at Permian High School for several years," I answered. "I guess you can call me that."

"I was just telling the boys that MOJO stuff you ran out there in West Texas ain't gonna work here in Clarksville," he told me. "These kids don't know how to win. You can't come out here with that MOJO stuff and win with these kids."

I let him finish with his assessment. I could tell he was putting on a show for his boys at the table. They were all listening and watching intently.

"Sir," I said, "if I believed these kids couldn't win, I wouldn't be here."

I walked past him and left.

After that conversation in the convenience store, our team won the next three ball games. The players, the kids at the schools, and the town went into a feeding frenzy. Everybody wanted to be a part of the action.

On Thursdays, I had a class at SMU. I drove 150 miles to Dallas and then back to Clarksville each Thursday for Thursday's pre-game meeting. After we won those three games in a row, the players' spirits had been high. But on the following Thursday when I returned, the team was in turmoil. During a video session of our practice, one of the managers filming the practice had referred to me as a "nigger."

His exact words were, "Look at that nigger's eyes!"

During the filming of the practice, he forgot the volume was turned on. As the coaching staff and the players watched the video they heard his comment. Apparently, when I was coaching during intense moments something unique must have happened with my eyes that truly astounded him. He was really excited about it.

The minute I walked into the field house I could tell something was different. The head coach called me to his office and explained the situation in detail. He said that the black players, who made up about half the team, were upset over the comment. He asked me how I wanted to handle the situation, and added that he would definitely have the manager extend me an apology.

This was nothing new. Race relations between blacks and whites in East Texas and West Texas were compatible.

"Coach, this is no big thing," I told him. "I've been here before."

## Segregated Seating

Following the very first game of that season, my wife had asked me if I knew that seating at the stadium was segregated. She had sat with the head coach's wife, who was white, during the game and had noticed whites sitting on one side of the divide and blacks on the other side.

The head coach's wife told Callie that it was going to cause a stir that she sat on the whites' side. After Callie pointed it out to me, I did notice a partition that extended from the top to the bottom of the seating area. I had thought nothing of it when I first saw it. This was 1996, and segregation hadn't entered my mind. But I said to Callie, "I'm not going to worry about that. I'm here to coach football on Friday nights and preach the gospel on Sunday mornings."

I had the best job in the town.

I told the head coach I would address the team just before practice on Monday. I was experiencing the same problem I had encountered in Odessa, where the black players were using the "N" word with each other, and with their white teammates.

When I addressed the team, I told them I appreciated their being upset about this situation, but that I was a bit confused as to why they would be upset. With the whole team sitting in front of me, I particularly and specifically addressed the black players. I asked them, "Why would you be upset about it when you're using the "N" word every day in the locker room? This whole situation is about two things—character and respect. The picture of your character that you paint for your teammates when you use the "N" word in their presence is one of no self-respect. And if you don't have self-respect as a man, you have nothing. They will never view you as a man of character when you do that. If you really want this issue to be addressed, stop using the "N" word and take pride in who you are and how you want to be addressed and respected as a man. Then, and only then, will issues concerning the use of this "N" word be addressed with any seriousness by me or any member of this coaching staff."

With that, the issue was dismissed and never mentioned again.

## Breaking Racial Barriers

Callie and I have spent a large portion of our lives being the only blacks in many situations during much of our employment history—first as individuals and later as a married couple. We never thought much about it, because our hearts have always been to serve to the best of our abilities.

When I became the pastor at St. Paul, we did the things we had always done. We invited the coaches and their wives, the players and their parents to events at the church and the worship services. Occasionally, they'd show up.

We never gave any thought to breaking racial barriers in the community. We were just doing the things we love to do. I was shopping at the local Walmart one day when a white player's mother approached me. I didn't know who she was, and I didn't know she worked there; I had never met her before.

She introduced herself, saying she was the mother of one of our players. Then, she became very emotional and began to cry. Through her tears, she said "Thank you for what you've done for my son. He thinks the world of you." She hugged me, and then whispered in my ear: "You don't know the impact you have on those boys and this community."

After that, she stepped back, looked me in the eyes, thanked me again, and walked away. The encounter left an impression on me.

Later, in January, when the football season concluded, we had our annual church conference and the superintendent from the Methodist Church was there. In his concluding remarks, he stated I had done more to break racial barriers in Clarksville than anyone had in the past fifty years. I was later informed that was the first time, in the history of that church, that whites had participated in a worship service.

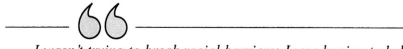

*I wasn't trying to break racial barriers; I was hoping to help the players build a relationship with Jesus.*

**An Amazing Season**

We won five games that year, and finished the season with a

record of 5-5, and played for a district championship. We lost the district championship 7-6 in a hard-fought battle against Pleasant Grove. I was really proud of the way our team played that game. We were out numbered and lost several key players to injury, but they never gave up. They fought hard to the very end. During the season, we even beat a team the school had lost to for ten consecutive years. It truly was an amazing season.

During the middle of the season, when we won those three games in a row, the superintendent and the president of the School Board approached me after a game. The superintendent said, "Coach, we would like to offer you the job as our head coach next year."

The school board president added: "We're not blind. We see why these kids are winning."

I was humbled by their offer. I enjoyed my time in Clarksville—pastoring the church and coaching the team—but I didn't accept the position.

At the beginning of the season, one of my assigned duties was to exhort the team during pre-game and halftime. I served as coach and chaplain for the team; it was a natural fit since I was the pastor of the local Methodist church.

During those times I looked in the players' eyes, and told them they had the same talent as the players on those Permian State Championship teams. But I could tell when I said it, they didn't believe me. They would drop their heads or their eyes would shift.

It was difficult, but I didn't stop encouraging them to put their faith in God, work hard, and develop a relationship with their Lord and Savior. I wanted them to know nothing was impossible with Jesus.

After the season, several of the players came by the

parsonage one day and asked if I had a moment to talk. We sat on the porch and talked about the season and the district championship game. Collectively, they told me if they had believed in what I was telling them at the very beginning of the season during those pre-game and halftime talks, they could have won all their games.

It was important for me to hear that. I could see in their eyes that the doubt and fear displayed at the beginning of the season was gone. They had become confident in their ability to win. The perceived disadvantage had been turned into an advantage that would have a transforming effect for life. When we beat the team we had lost to for ten consecutive years, I could see confidence start to build in their eyes.

Believing something can happen and being confident in an outcome are two totally different things and on that day, sitting on those steps listening to those young men and looking into their eyes, I came away with a deeper appreciation for what that mother said to me in Walmart.

Those young men had arrived. I do not believe my accepting the position as pastor of the church and coach of the football team was an accident. It was a divine appointment. In my opinion, that season transformed their lives. The eyes are the windows to the soul. They will reveal what God has placed on the heart.

A good leader opens the eyes of those in their charge to the possibilities that lay before them.

# PART 4:
# Your Legacy, Your Story

*Dr. Nathanial Hearne - Coach, teacher, and "character-builder" for many kids over the years.*

# Chapter 12
# What's Your Dash?

*"I always thought Bissinger's characterization of Coach Hearne was unfair and overly dismissive. I think Coach Hearne viewed his job as inspiring young people to greatness, and in particular part of that job was helping black athletes navigate the system, for the athlete's benefit. The other coaches may well have viewed Coach Hearne's job differently, but his personal motives were clear to those of us who trained under him—he was using the gifts and opportunities he had to raise up a new generation of great young people."*

-The New York Times College Sports Blog
September 10, 2008 by Wade[1]

Permian High School was, in my opinion, one of the finest institutions in this nation. There were many success stories I celebrated:

During my coaching career at Permian, I lost a total of eight games as an assistant coach. Some coaches lose that many in a season.

I assisted with several different junior varsity teams over the years that never lost a game—60-0-1.

In 1987, we had the smallest team in the state. Our middle linebacker weighed 140 lbs. The weakside and outside linebackers weighed 155 lbs. each. The defensive ends weighed 165 lbs. and the 2 Techniques weighed in at 175 lbs. We didn't have an offensive lineman who weighed more than 185 lbs. These young men won thirteen games on a 5-4A level! That's the stuff legends are made of. They felt there was not an opponent they faced who couldn't be beaten. They never gave up. They never, never, never quit! They displayed the kind of character during those games that made my heart swell with pride.

I also coached junior varsity basketball at Permian. One particular team I coached won thirty straight ball games, averaged ninety-eight points a game, and every player on the team played in every single ball game. That was an amazing group of talented young men.

I've traveled this country from the east coast to the west coast presenting on educational reforms. I have not been to one single city in America that didn't know Permian football. There are not many football programs in the state of Texas that can say that.

Coaching, teaching, and being a school administrator gave me the privilege of working with wonderful parents, outstanding dedicated teachers, and great coaches, which, to this day, I consider an honor.

The football program and what it did for the community, the students, the players, and the coaching staff, will never be equaled. The panther paw print it left on Odessa, the state of Texas, and this nation will never be forgotten.

In chapter 3, I talked about the importance of the kind of legacy we, as parents, coaches, teachers, and individuals, should leave. Let me end this book by sharing with you a brief story, and an illustration of what leaving a legacy means to me.

When we die, there will be a tombstone placed on top of our graves. The engraving on that tombstone will include our date of birth, a dash, and the date we died. I'd like you to think the dash represents your legacy.

If you have a discerning spirit, God will often give you a snapshot of your legacy. It comes in some of the strangest places, at some of the strangest times.

Not long ago a Fuzzy's Taco Shop opened near the area where I worked. Obviously, the restaurant quickly became the rave, because cars were lined up for as much as two miles to wait for service. It was there that God gave me a glimpse of my legacy.

Not wanting to fight the crowd, I waited until almost 3 o'clock to go to lunch. When I walked inside the restaurant, two college-age ladies were taking orders. As I stepped up to order, one of the girls said politely, "Hi, Mr. Hearne."

Realizing I didn't recognize who she was, she said, "You wouldn't know me, but you were my principal when I was in high school. I never got in any trouble to be sent to your office."

Smiling, I said to her: "That's kind of bittersweet. I'm glad you didn't get in any trouble to be sent to my office, but it saddens me to know that I never got the opportunity to know you." She smiled, and asked if I were still a principal at the school. I responded that I was now the Student Attendance Specialist for the district.

Then, the other girl spoke up.

"You're the one who goes out and writes tickets, and harasses students into coming to school," she said.

"No, that's not what we do," I responded. "My officers conference with the families about the problems, and I find resources to help them. We want to avoid writing citations."

As I was explaining this to her, I could see the young lady who knew me as her principal was smiling. When I finished explaining, she said: "Mr. Hearne, that's what you've always done. You've always tried to help people."

"Sweetie," I said, "I need your name and your phone number. Don't worry, it's all good. I want you to preach my eulogy when I die. My wife will call you on that day. You don't have to prepare anything. When time comes for the eulogy, you step to the pulpit and say, 'Mr. Hearne always tried to help people.' And you can sit back down. That's all you have to say."

That's my dash. It's all I want people to remember about me—that I always tried to help people.

Ecclesiastes 7:1 reads, "*A good name is better than precious ointment, and the day of death [is better] than the day of birth.*" *(ESV)*

What does your dash represent?

When your life is centered on helping young people achieve success, they'll let you know if you're on the right track or not. The following e-mails and Facebook messages are from children of friends and former students I've had the great fortune and opportunity to work and interact with over the years to help them think differently and not accept the conventional order of things.

**An e-mail from Fonzell O. Veale, former Permian student; sent on August 28, 2011, 2:24 p.m.:**

"Mr. Hearne, it is with great joy and excitement that I write to inform you that your kindness, grace, and stern example was not in vain during your years at PHS. You were my AP during my junior year, which was a very troublesome year for me. You invited my father and I to hear you preach because you knew I needed more than what was being offered at PHS. I believe that was your final year at PHS and I was able to pull myself together enough to graduate the following year.

"Since then I have worked with youth in many different arenas. My journey has taken me clear across the country. I have been in NC for the past 10 years and finally graduated from college in 2008. I have been in education for 7 years and currently am in my 4th year as a Behavior Support teacher.

"I often tell my students and others about your influence on my life. You led by example and made critical decisions that had a direct impact on my life. You are without a doubt one of the main reasons I chose a career in education. You also showed me that a real man needs to be spiritually strong and make decisions based on Godly principles.

"It does not surprise me to hear that you have continued to do great things after leaving PHS. Sandi Omerod sees you in the same light that I see you—you are a great man that has positively impacted the world.

"I pray that this message reaches you in great health and prosperity. And, may the God of heaven and earth continue to bless your family as you press forward with great work!"

Fonzell O. Veale | PHS class of '96

**Facebook message from April, former PHS student; sent April 18, 2013, 6:25 p.m.:**

"I'm dying...I just came across your name on Facebook...it's so good to see you well. I sure hope you and your family are doing good. I've thought about you often and the great influence you had on my life. So good to come across your name and face. Happy Birthday!"

**Facebook message from Mikala, former PHS student; sent May 15, 2013, 9:20 a.m.:**

"Hi Coach Hearne! I clearly remember a valuable lesson you taught as my class principal. I wanted to be anywhere besides sitting in your office at Permian. I was called in for extreme tardiness/questionable truancy after registering for dual-credit at the community college. It's most ironic I'm now faculty at that same college! Never know where one's path will lead! So nice to see you on fb!"

**Facebook message from Chad, former PHS student; sent November 8, 2013, 10:19 p.m.:**

"Coach Hearne, good to see you sir! I was with you at PHS back in 1988-90. I always respected, looked up to you and valued your coaching. I pray all is well for you and thank you for all you did for us at Permian."

**Facebook message from Bill, former PHS student; sent April 14, 2013, 9:07 p.m.:**

"Do not know if you remember me but I will never forget about you. You were my coach back in the early 90s. You have always been a big inspiration to me and I will never forget you Coach Hearne."

**Facebook message from Robert, a friend's son; sent May 23, 2013, 11:39 p.m.:**

"Hello Mr. Hearne… Thank you for adding me as a friend… Do you remember who I am…You are still looking young…It will be great to catch up!! Everything is well with my family…I'm married and we have three children…Are you still in Texas? I'm just a few hours away the next time I'm there I would really love to see you!! You really had a great impact on my life. I really appreciate you!"

**Facebook message from Jason, former PHS student; sent January 9, 2012, 12:35 a.m.:**

"I don't know if you remember me or not Mr. Hearne, I thoroughly enjoyed your Biology class while I was at Permian. I knew not to get on your bad side, but you also quietly taught me that anything was possible with a little bit of hard work and some elbow grease. Funny how you never remember anything learned from a book and yet you remember the life lessons people have taught you many years later. I hope God has blessed you these past few years and I hope you are well. Thanks again for giving me the ability to believe in myself no matter what situation I found myself in."

**Facebook message from Shannon, former PHS student; sent February 2, 2011, 1:16 p.m.:**

"Is this Coach Hearne that taught at Permian? Thank you for the response! I hope all is well with you and your family. We are wonderful on this end as well! I have thought about you many times over the years, you were a true blessing to me in high school and I will never forget you."

**Facebook message from Matthew, former PHS student; sent August 28, 2013, 6:44 p.m.:**

"Sir did you ever teach biology at Permian High School? Do you remember taking a young man out in the hallway and asking him why he was wasting his time and not pursuing more challenging courses? It was a driving force in my life. I wanted to thank you and apologize for not taking your advice right then. I recently retired a decorated Marine and I got a college degree with a 3.975 GPA. Thank you, sir. I will never forget that day. God bless you."

**This letter was written by Kathy Keeton to the principal at Permian H.S. following the incident I referenced in Chapter 9 regarding her son, Nick:**

"I want you to know how very much I appreciate Mr. Nate

Hearne. On Monday of this week I had a visit with Mr. Hearne regarding a problem. Not only did Mr. Hearne allow me as much time as I needed to 'wring my hands,' he immediately found the best solution for my child and took care of it. I left Permian that afternoon feeling secure in the fact that I have a voice when I have a concern, and if possible, acted upon. The most important feeling I have is that my child is important to Mr. Hearne. This is not because he might know him, but that Mr. Hearne's first concern is the kids. I am so impressed and thankful.

"I am grateful that my child, and all of the junior class, will have Mr. Hearne as their junior and senior principal to stand with them through their next two years.

Sincerely,

Kathy Keeton"

In his book *David and Goliath*, Malcolm Gladwell speaks of the advantages of disadvantages and the disadvantages of perceived advantages. We often operate under the perceived assumption that superior height, weight, wealth, or intelligence gives a person a huge advantage.[2]

But what I've taught for years to students all across Texas is don't ever consent defeat until you've made your opponent earn it. Don't ever look across the classroom or athletic field and think other students are better than you because they are smarter or bigger. Be that person who doesn't always accept the conventional order of thinking.

When Jesus said in Matthew 3:2: *"Repent, for the kingdom of heaven has come near," (HCSB)* I do not believe He was talking about our sins. I believe Jesus was asking us to think differently about how we perceive things. He wanted us to know that we have the ability to turn any disadvantage into an advantage.

In John 14:12 Jesus said, *"Very truly I tell you, whoever believes in me will do the works that I have been doing, and they will do even greater things than these, because I am going to the Father."* (NIV)

He wanted us to know we have the ability to do the impossible if we change the way we think about perceived disadvantages.

Jesus left us with an advocate to give us confidence to think and act differently when we face perceived disadvantages. In John 14:26 Jesus said, *"The Counselor, the Holy Spirit–the Father will send Him in My name–will teach you all things and remind you of everything I have told you."* (HCSB)

Character is not something that can be bought; it has to be developed. And that development can only come as a result of training. Leaders, you are charged with training those in your care. Leading often gets confused with dictating, micro-managing, yelling orders, or pushing people around. When that's the case, I believe the leader is more focused on secular goals than on God's goals.

66

*Training is what Jesus did during the time He spent with His disciples. He wanted to leave them something they could live by. Not only that, He wanted to impart something they could pass on to their children, and their children's children for generations to come.*

99

Jesus spent His entire time here on earth teaching, coaching, and training everyone He came in contact with. He did it with selfless love, and a desire to see people changed. Jesus wanted to instill in His disciples the values of bearing fruit of character: love, humility, compassion, forgiveness, and service. Yes, character can be taught. Who is going to step up and take ownership to teach it? How do you want to be remembered? What will your legacy be?

You have it within you to lead anyone God puts in your path, and to overcome any obstacle or enemy. I say this with confidence, and if you remember nothing else from this work, I want you to remember that the One who is in you is greater than any opponent you will ever face.

# References

Introduction
    [1]Nathanial Hearne, "A Wesleyan Rule of Life" (A Professional Project Submitted to The Faculty of Perkins School of Theology) Dallas, Texas, 2009

Chapter 1
    [1]H.G. Bissinger, *Friday Night Lights* (Massachusetts, Da Capo Press, 1990), 262-263
    [2 3]Paul Tough, *How Children Succeed* (New York, Houghton Mifflin Harcourt, 2012), 7, 58

Chapter 2
    [1]H.G. Bissinger, *Friday Night Lights* (Massachusetts, Da Capo Press, 1990), 263

Chapter 3
    [1 2]http://thequad.blogs.nytimes.com/2008/09/08

Chapter 4
    [1]Garry Leavell, "Battle Leaves Scars on Both Sides of Fight" (*Odessa American*, September 21, 1990)
    [2]Gaylon Krisak and Garry Leavell, "District says Permian guilty of violations" (*Odessa American,* September 11, 1990)
    [3]Minutes obtained from the State of Texas University Interscholastic League Executive Committee Meeting held September 20, 1990, at Radisson Hotel, Austin, Texas. (Item BB)

Chapter 5
    [1]Garry Leavell, "Investigations Aren't Over Yet" (*Odessa American,* September 21, 1990)

Chapter 6
    [1]H.G. Bissinger, *Friday Night Lights* ( Massachusetts, Da Capo Press, 1990), 108

Chapter 7
    [1]Malcolm Gladwell, *David and Goliath* (New York, Little, Brown and Company, 2013), 25

Chapter 8
    [1]Joe Ehrmann, *InSideOut* Coaching (New York, Simon & Schuster, 2011), 12

Chapter 9
    [1]H.G. Bissinger, *Friday Night Lights* (Massachusetts, Da Capo Press, 1990), 104-105

Chapter 10
    [1]Dale Carnegie, *How to Stop Worrying and Start Living* (Great Britain, The Chaucer Press, 1948)

Chapter 11
    [1]Paul Tough, *How Children Succeed* (New York, Houghton Mifflin Harcourt, 2012)

Chapter 12
    [1]http://thequad.blogs.nytimes.com/2008/09/08
    [2]Malcolm Gladwell, *David and Goliath* (New York: Little, Brown and Company, 2013)

# About the Author

Dr. Hearne is the Assistant Executive Director of the Greater Dallas/Ft. Worth Fellowship of Christian Athletes. He served as an assistant principal at L.D. Bell High School in Hurst, Texas for four years, and as assistant principal of the Discipline Alternative Education Program for five years. His last five years in the district, he served as the Student Attendance Specialist and Director over the Hurst-Euless-Bedford Independent School District's Truancy Department.

Dr. Hearne came to the Hurst-Euless-Bedford area from the Ector County Independent School District, where he worked for 18 years as a science teacher, coach, and administrator. While in Ector County, he was an assistant coach for the Permian High School football team, which won the 1989 State and National Championship and the 1991 State Championship. (Permian High School became the subject of the book *Friday Night Lights* and the subsequent movie and TV series by the same name).

In 1988, Dr. Hearne was named as an assistant to coach the North All-Star Football Team. Dr. Hearne was named Outstanding Principal of the Year for Region 18 for the Ector County Independent School District in 1993-94, and Assistant Principal of the Year for the Hurst-Euless-Bedford Independent School District in 2008.

Dr. Hearne has served as pastor of several small Methodist churches over the past fifteen years.

In his duties as Assistant Director of DFWFCA, he conducts the pre-game chapel services for several university football teams, including University of Oklahoma, Texas Christian University, University of Tulsa, University of Idaho, University of Indiana and Louisiana Tech.

In December of 2010, the Dropout Prevention Program Dr. Hearne initiated in the HEBISD was recognized by Texas School Business magazine as the best dropout prevention program in the state.

Dr. Hearne is married to Callie, a recently retired Assistant Superintendent over the Human Resource Department for the Hurst-Euless-Bedford Independent School District. They have five children and three grandchildren and presently reside in Arlington, Texas.

Dr. Hearne's passion is to mentor and build up leadership skills in others, particularly those who have direct influence on the lives of youth. He is a sought-after keynote speaker and workshop leader for kids or youth gatherings, graduations, men's conferences, coaching, and leadership events. His engaging, straight-forward manner, combined with his heart for building character, leaves his audience inspired to be better, live with purpose, and accept their calling. To contact Dr. Hearne, reach him through his website:

www.NateHearne.com

# RESOURCES

## Study Guide

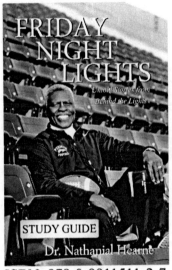

ISBN: 978-0-9911511-2-7

This 7-week study is for anyone who wants to not only grow deeper in God's Word, but also develop leadership skills.

By taking his personal principles for excellence and expanding on what he presents in his book, Dr. Hearne helps you see not only how you can build into your own character, but also become a mentor and leader who builds into the lives of others.

## DVD

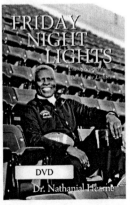

ISBN: 978-0-9911511-4-1

Dr. Hearne shares more of his experiences and philosophies for building biblical success in this DVD teaching.

Includes live teaching that compliments the Study Guide and testimonies from students who worked with Dr. Hearne during his years at Permian.

CPSIA information can be obtained at www.ICGtesting.com
Printed in the USA
LVOW10s0327190314

377990LV00001B/1/P